Thomas Chalmers Minor

Athothis

A Satire on Modern Medicine

Thomas Chalmers Minor

Athothis
A Satire on Modern Medicine

ISBN/EAN: 9783337779061

Printed in Europe, USA, Canada, Australia, Japan

Cover: Foto ©Thomas Meinert / pixelio.de

More available books at **www.hansebooks.com**

A SATIRE ON MODERN MEDICINE

BY

THOMAS C. MINOR

"I believe that all that use sorceries, incantations, and spells, are not witches, or, as we term them, magicians. I conceive there is a traditional magick, not learned immediately from the devil, but at second-hand from his scholars. who having once the secret betrayed, do empirically practice without his advice."—*Religio Medici.*

———————

CINCINNATI
ROBERT CLARKE & CO
1887

This Little Volume is Dedicated

TO

DR. JOHN S. BILLINGS,

Assistant Surgeon-General of the United States Army,

by his old-time friend and admirer,

THE AUTHOR.

(3)

TABLE OF CONTENTS.

(v)

ATHOTHIS:

A SATIRE ON MODERN MEDICINE.

CHAPTER I.

INTRODUCES DOCTOR PAULUS ANDROCYDES AND HIS PET
CAT ANUBIS.

HE cathedral bells were chiming the hour of
midnight, yet Doctor Paulus Androcydes still
lingered over a roll of papyrus and slowly de-
ciphered the curious hieroglyphics. On an
oriental rug in front of an open grate, filled with red
coals, sat an enormous Angora cat, which seemed to be
enjoying the heat radiated from the burning embers. A
lamp of antique pattern, suspended from the ceiling by
copper chains, threw a mysterious light over the spec-
tacled student, and defined the various objects around it
with peculiar distinctness.

In each corner of the apartment hung carved oaken
brackets, shaped in imitation of the Egyptian lotus, sym-
bolic of life eternal. Poised on each of these supports
was a stuffed bird; on one a hawk, the hieroglyphic for
the soul, sacred to Horus; on another a lapwing, typical
of the solar period, the return of Osiris to life; on a
third an ibis, or crane, significant of intelligence; on a
fourth, a swallow with outstretched wings. The ceiling

was painted deep blue, ornamented by a single silver star, or Isis in heaven. The walls were covered by a paper of unique design, the frieze representing a mass of writhing green serpents with ruby eyes; the dado, brown monkeys stretching long hairy arms, and climbing the branches of a banyan tree; the open space between frieze and dado was filled with a floral design composed of fig leaves, Balanites Ægyptica—the sacred heart of Horus, and the trefoil—emblem of the three in one mystery, or Egyptian trinity.

In one corner of the room rested a large sarcophagus, with its hideous lid removed and leaning against the wall, while within this ancient burial casket reclined a swaddled mummy from the necropolis of Memphis. A low table, covered with retorts, test tubes, chemicals in bottles, human bones, a grinning white skull, morbid anatomical specimens in alcohol, and a microscope, stood in the center of the apartment. A few leather-covered chairs, studded with huge brass nails, were scattered around; and the only remaining nooks were filled by large walnut book-cases, containing musty-looking tomes bound in parchment, the titles of which were delicately marked on the back in the blackest of India ink. The works of Hippocrates, Galen, Rhazes, and Avicenna were particularly noticeable in this collection.

The oddest of all the oddities visible, however, was Doctor Paulus Androcydes, physician, chemist, Egyptologist, delver in the occult sciences, investigator of all eastern mysteries. Seated at one end of the study table, with his huge blue goggles protruding from each side of a very prominent nose, his head, even at a short distance, resembled that of a gigantic Arctic owl—this effect being heightened by an abundant suit of bushy hair of snowy whiteness. A receding and almost undeveloped chin added to his bird-like aspect. Exceedingly thin, with rounded and almost hump-like shoulders, grasping the papyrus with long lean fingers that looked like talons more than human hands, his shadow, projected by the firelight, was an exact counterpart of the bird of wisdom. His age might have been fifty years, but he could have passed for a man of seventy. Attired in a dressing-gown of black velvet, with a quilted satin lining apparent at the wristbands and collar; his pantaloons, visible under the table, were lavender colored; while, covering his really small feet, were red silk stockings encased in patent leather slippers.

The last stroke of the chimes had scarcely died away, when the cat arose, and, stretching its body in the usual feline manner, looked around for a moment, then, with a gentle purr, approached its master's chair. This movement, on the part of his pet, did not seem to disturb the doctor, for he still continued to pore over the ancient document. After making a few caressing circles around the physician's legs in the evident hope of attracting attention—a hope that remained unrealized, the cat suddenly sprang upon the table, and in performing this act of agility overturned the white skull, which fell to the floor with a sharp ominous crack. This secured the desired effect, for Doctor Paulus Androcydes looked up from the papyrus in evident surprise and dismay; then, murmuring in an expostulating tone, "Why do you annoy me, Anubis?" he moved back his chair, yawned, glanced at the ticking clock on the mantel, rose and walked to the window, which he opened.

The cool air fanned his face, and seemed to revive and arouse the physician, for he yawned again like a person just awakened, stretched his arms, and then peered out into the night. From his elevated apartment he saw the many roofs of houses and the tall chimneys outlined in silhouette against the clear sky. In the streets below all was solemn silence. Turning his eyes from scenes terrestrial to things celestial, the doctor closely scanned the heavens and gazed intently at the moon, as that bright luminary seemed to shine with more than its usual resplendence, and its silvery disc cast a collection of brilliant rays directly on his uncovered head, enveloping it in a halo of glory. At this moment he must have been moon-struck, as his lips moved, and he remarked, aloud: "I do not believe it! Transmigration? nonsense!" and withdrew from the window. Then, walking to the fireplace, turned his back to the agreeable heat, and again commenced musing.

Doctor Paulus Androcydes was thinking of the wonderful papyrus lying there on his study table, and the mysteries it revealed—mysteries as old as Chaldea and Egypt—revelations regarding ancient charms and incantations—instructions in magic and the black arts—essays on fairies, gnomes, witches, and spirits—the relations of physical to astral life—a veritable treatise on sciences and arts that the present world has forgotten, but will sometime rediscover and proclaim as new. In addition to all this valuable information, the papyrus included an appendix concerning the performance of miracles in medical practice, and furnished cabalistical formulæ for the making of health-giving philters and disease-preventing amulets. Strangest of all contained in the scroll, however, was the strong argument advanced in favor of the doctrine of metempsychosis.

Doctor Paulus Androcydes was deeply versed in the

literature of by-gone epochs; he had studied the works of Trismegistus, Zeno, Hippocrates, Epictetus, and Xenocrates. He had pondered over Pythagorean theories and laughed at the strange conceits as to spirits and devils held by Paracelsus; yet, he had never believed that the soul of Euphorbus had transmigrated to Lucian's chicken. His library was filled with the most antiquated editions of the philosophers and scientists of former centuries from which he had appropriated the choicest extracts of ancient wisdom; but now, there confronted him that most obsolete of all writings, an Egyptian papyrus. Before this scroll of the earliest dynasty the authors of the classical Greek and Latin periods seemed modern.

There was an audacity about this Egyptian writer that inspired wonder on the part of the reader; his views were very pleasing on account of their originality; his statements were clear and concise; he indulged in no theories, and made no reference to other works; what he wrote was stated as fact, fixed and immutable as the laws governing the universe. Either the author of these hieroglyphical lines was the colossal prevaricator of his age or he possessed supernatural powers; for he professed ability to restore disembodied spirits to their former human habitations, provided certain conditions were complied with, and claimed that any physician, following the instructions laid down in the manuscript, could produce the same marvelous results.

Doctor Paulus Androcydes was an extremely skeptical man, yet, in the present instance, the perusal of this papyrus had made an impression such as he had never before experienced. He was irritated beyond measure for even dreaming for a moment that there was the least probability in any of the Egyptian writer's statements; hence his condemnatory exclamation, "Transmigration? nonsense!" So he stood in front of the fire-place biting his lips in vexation that any doubt should still linger in his mind, until, attracted by an uncontrollable impulse, he again approached the table and taking up the manuscript reread the first passage that fell under his vision, which was as follows:

"All atoms are eternal!

" The earth is composed of an aggregation of atoms : it follows that man who is of the earth is likewise eternal.

"Atoms may exist in a state of aggregation or segregation.

" The aggregation of atoms is the result of the action of fire, air, and water. Their segregation is caused by the same forces.

" Now, fire is Ra, the glorious Sun God; the air is Shu, the son of Ra; the earth is Seb, the son of Shu; while the water is Osiris, the son of Seb. These four divinities, acting in unity, produce all living matter; but such action can not be induced save through Patah, the father of all the gods and creator of life; he alone is the divine essence. The divine essence is eternal. It may pass from one aggregation to another as it wills. When present it is called life : when absent the atoms return to Seb, the earth which gave them.

"Aggregations of atoms assume different forms; but the essence called life remains the same forever, although passing from one shape to another. The divine essence that existed centuries since in that form of aggregated atoms called man may exist to-day in the shape of a cat, that animal sacred to the Lunar deities.

" It is only by the aid of Patah, father of all the gods,

that mankind, his children, parts of the divine essence, maintain that most beautiful and primal type of creation, the human body.

"Through the intervention of Patah, this divine essence, after undergoing many transmigrations, may be made to re-enter its original form of aggregated atoms, providing these atoms formed from Seb, the earth, have been preserved in their original external shape. To perform this miracle we must first discover the exact aggregation in which the divine essence of a former mortal has its present abode. It may be that it permeates an animal, bird, fish, insect, or plant.

"Now, I, Athothis, son of Mena, founder of the Egyptian line of kings, when chief physician, astrologer, and magician to my father's court, was taught the incantations and processes necessary for the performance of this miracle by certain wise seers and necromancers from Chaldea, and upon at least three occasions have given life by restoring the vital essence to mummies which had laid embalmed in tombs for over five hundred years. These same incantations may be done by any man learned in the wisdom of ancient Egypt; and if this person be a skilled physican, versed in anatomy, he can easily apply the methods to be followed."

Doctor Paulus Androcydes again laid down the papyrus and indulged in a low, gurgling, disdainful laugh; then speaking aloud to himself, as was his custom when alone, he said, " Oh! Athothis, son of Mena, Ananias was the embodiment of truth when compared to thee!"

He had scarcely spoken these scornful words when the cat gave a blood-curdling scream of anger, and the physician arose to his feet in astonishment and dismay; for there, on the table, stood Anubis with his back curved and every hair on end, his tail elevated and swollen to twice its natural size, while his eyes, expanded like those of a raging demon or furious goblin, emitted brilliant phosphorescent flashes of light, intelligent gleams of indignant protest.

Quickly recovering from the fright induced by this strange manifestation of wrath on the part of a heretofore amiable pet, Doctor Paulus Androcydes cried out in a conciliatory, apologetic voice, "Forgive my rude remark, Anubis, thou very prince of cats; for if the divine essence of Athothis, greatest of all Egyptian magi, resides in thee, most grievous has been my offense, and I humbly crave pardon!"

The mere utterance of these words seemed to exert a magical effect on the cat, for its tail resumed a normal size, its fur became smooth and glossy, while the savage eyes again assumed their wonted expression of tender regard. As the doctor saw this sudden change in the aspect of the animal, he sank back in a softly-cushioned reclining chair, perfectly overcome with astonishment. In the meantime, Anubis walked up and down the table, purring in a most affectionate manner.

A flood of curious ideas and fancies filled the mind of Doctor Paulus Androcydes, foremost among which was the thought that perhaps, after all, the doctrine of metempsychosis was not entirely false. Who knew but that this very cat might contain the essence of life that once inhabited the body of Athothis?

Who was Athothis? The papyrus lying there was certainly genuine; for only that morning he had taken the scroll from the burial casket resting in the corner. He was sure that the ancient sarcophagus had never been tampered with, inasmuch as it had been obtained at an extravagant price from an Arab sheik, through the American consul at Alexandria, who had forwarded with it a certificate, duly signed and adorned with many seals, stating that the mummy was several thousand years old, and remained in the same condition as when found. What if the mummy so quietly reclining there was the author of this hieroglyphical writing? What if the cat was now the abode of Athothis? Here was the rarest opportunity ever offered a savant of the nineteenth century to test the marvelous experiment of a necromancer who had lived centuries before; and most fitting conclusion of all, this test could be applied to the very individual who had asserted the possession of what seemed to be supernatural power; for if the mummy were really the Egyptian author, and his spirit had transmigrated until it now resided in Anubis, it would be a simple matter, according to the directions laid down in the papyrus, to restore a disembodied spirit to its original human habitation.

Doctor Paulus Androcydes trembled violently with nervous agitation as he pondered over the subject, and his excited brain was almost overcome by a violent congestion. He grew faint and dizzy. Staggering from his chair, he supported his feeble limbs by holding to the wall until he reached a book-case. Here he stretched out his hand toward an upper shelf, and taking down a small cut-glass flagon of antique design, filled with an amber-colored cordial, he withdrew the crystal stopper, and placing the flask to his mouth, swallowed a large quantity of the stimulating liquid. The cordial revived him almost immediately; a cheerful glow spread over his entire body, and he felt like a strong young man, with the will and energy necessary to overcome any ordinary physical or mental obstacle.

CHAPTER II.

DOCTOR PAULUS ANDROCYDES PERFORMS ONE OF THE MIRA-
CLES OF THE EGYPTIAN MAGI, AND RAISES THE SPIRIT
OF ATHOTHIS.

PPROACHING the sarcophagus, Doctor Paulus
Androcydes leaned over it meditatively for a
few seconds, then tenderly lifted out the
swaddled mummy, and, carrying it in his arms,
deposited the burden on the oriental rug in front of
the fire-place. Gently brushing off the brown dust
of ages that had accumulated on the external wrappings,
he took a sharp scalpel from an instrument case, and,
inserting it under one of the linen folds, made an incision outward; seizing the edge of the covering with the
finger-nails of his right hand, he proceeded to unwrap
the shroud, turning over the mummy again and again as
he unrolled layer after layer of the bitumen-saturated
fabric. Several times, small bunches of Balanites Ægyptica dropped to the floor, and, on the first instant's exposure to air, crumbled into ashes. In the meantime,
Anubis walked up and down the table, watching his master and mewing uneasily. Finally, the doctor pulled off
the last covering, and the hideous, black, shrunken body
of the mummy lay exposed in all its nakedness, while
over its right side extended the rude gashing opening
through which the ancient embalmers had withdrawn the
viscera. This aperture was partially closed by an emblem representing the sacred eye of Horus, god of the

early dawn—typifying the resurrection, the return of light from darkness. As the physician withdrew this emblem, a horrible cry of feline agony resounded through the room, and turning in terror he beheld his pet cat lying on the floor, frothing at the mouth in a frightful convulsion.

The first impulse of Doctor Paulus Androcydes was to relieve the cat of pain, and running to the book-case he grasped a vial labeled chloroform, and quickly poured a quantity of this powerful anæsthetic on a sponge. While thus employed, Anubis seemed to revive, and dragged himself up to the mummy's side, where, resting his head on the embalmed remains, he moaned and wailed, while large tears rolled down his furry cheeks. The cat's grief seemed almost human.

"The Egyptian author's words are true!" gasped the physician—snatching up the papyrus and perusing it intently—"I shall apply the tests immediately." And with this he read aloud the directions laid down in the scroll of Athothis, which were as follows:

"In order to restore life to its original habitation, it is absolutely necessary to incinerate that animal in which the divine essence has its present abode.

"The ashes left after incineration must be for the most part collected and placed in the body of the mummy through the opening made by the evisceraters or embalmers, professionally known as Parachistes. At the first moment of incineration this incantation is to be solemnly pronounced:

"'Oh! Ra, glorious God of the Sun! Immortal Creator of fire! In the name of Patah—thy divine father—I invoke thy power! Drive out from this aggregation of atoms all the divine essence which now lingers within, and restore life to its original dwelling-place.'

"As he repeats this invocation, the necromancer must bow to the east—toward the rising sun—concluding with these words:

"'I command thy aid in the name of Horus and the blessed resurrection!'"

As he finished these lines, Doctor Paulus Androcydes dropped the manuscript, and stepping forward, without an instant's hesitation, seized Anubis and tightly wound the cat in some of the bitumen-soaked shroud taken from the mummy; then cast the bundle and its living inmate on the red-hot embers of the grate; afterward securing the front of the fire-place with a metallic blower. He now paused, and anxiously awaited developments.

There was a momentary silence, followed by a terrific roaring noise, as the resinous mummy wrappings were devoured by the flames. Suddenly, sweet strains of music floated over the room—stringed instruments, horns and cymbals uniting in melodious harmony, as though some angelic orchestra had broken forth in a magnificent triumphal hymn. At the same instant, joyful chattering voices were heard, and the delicious perfume of flowers seemed to be shed from a myriad of tender blossoms. The physician turned in wonder and awe at the strange spectacle revealed to his vision; for there, against the wall, climbing up and down the branches of the banyan tree on the dado, were dozens of brown monkeys playfully calling to each other; above were thousands of beautiful flowers, apparently nodding to the cadence of some mysterious and unfelt breeze; on the frieze were hundreds of serpents, turning and twisting in graceful contortions—their bodies changing colors like iridescent opals, while their ruby eyes flashed like myriads of scarlet sparks. Overhead, in place of the ceiling, appeared what seemed to be the firmament of heaven, in whose center shone the dog-star, Sirius, with its sparkling, diamond-like rays.

For a moment, but only for a moment, Doctor Paulus Androcydes stood in amazement, then realizing that time was precious, he read aloud the incantation. The music increased in volume; the chatter of the monkeys became deafening; while the odor of flowers grew as dense as the fragrance of a hundred censers.

A perfect mental calmness now succeeded the physician's previous nervous agitation, and all unmindful of the strangeness of the manifestations occurring, he continued to read the directions of the papyrus.

"After the incineration of the animal has been perfectly accomplished and the incantation duly performed, the sacred sepulchral vases or canopi, found in the sarcophagus, are to be removed and placed in a row at the mummy's right side. These canopi are to be arranged in the following order: first, the urn representing a man's head, which contains the stomach and large intestine belonging to the remains; this urn is guarded by the genius Amset; next, the urn in the form of the head of a cynocephalus ape, which contains the small intestine; this urn is watched over by the genius Hapis; next in order, the urn shaped like a jackal's head, which holds the heart and lungs; this urn is protected by the genius Snouf; finally, the urn in the likeness of a hawk's head, which contains the mummy's liver and gall bladder; this urn is defended by the genius Kebhousnouf. Having

2

placed these canopi in the order named, the necromancer
shall take a long inspiration and breathe on the urns separately. Then, this invocation is to be reverently repeated.

"Oh! Shu, God of the Air! Breather of life into all
living creatures! I invoke thy aid, in the name of Patah
the divine father. Restore to these lifeless organs the
vitality, strength, and movement necessary to perform
their functions. Oh! protecting genii! Amset, Hapis,
Snouf, and Kebhousnouf, I command thee all to release
thy charges!

"Then bowing to the east three times, the necromancer shall break the canopi and insert their contents
in the incision on the mummy's side."

Doctor Paulus Androcydes laid down the papyrus, and
going to the sarcophagus secured therefrom the urns,
and taking each one separately placed them in the order
named; first breathing on them the warm breath of life,
then he recited the incantation, and bowed three times to
the Orient.

The roaring in the fire-place and chimney had now
ceased; the strains of music in the air were growing
softer and more distant; the perfume of the flowers was
less dense but more delicate; while the chattering brown
monkeys relapsed into silence.

The physician removed the red-hot blower from the
grate, and saw that the work of incineration was complete—what had once been his pet cat was reduced to a
small mass of pearly pink ashes; removing this on a brass
shovel, he emptied the now incinerated dust of Anubis into
the opening on the mummy's side; then breaking the
canopi he introduced their contents through the same

aperture. Going to the table he once more picked up the scroll of Athothis, and read:

" To restore the disembodied spirit to its original habitation and give back to the body the natural motions and actions of life, fresh water must be sprinkled over the mummy with the necromancer's left hand, and this invocation solemnly intoned:

" Oh! Osiris! God of the Water! Sublime ruler of Amento, the silent land beyond the setting sun. I invoke thy assistance in returning the spirit belonging to these remains, in the name of Patah, Grand Master of the Universe; in the name of Horus, thy avenging son, I command the spiritual resurrection of this body!

"As the necromancer finishes this invocation, he shall take the emblem of life, which has previously been drawn from the mummy's side, and striking the remains with this symbol of Horus, shall cry aloud, 'In the name of Patah, Ra, Shu, Seb, and Osiris! I command thee to walk!' Then shall the mummy arise and walk; then shall the body once clothed with mortality be immortal— inhabited by a deity, with the powers of a God, making himself visible or invisible at will, and able to perform miracles."

Doctor Paulus Androcydes now filled a quaintly ornamented silver goblet with water, and kneeling at the mummy's side he sprinkled it over the remains, he slowly intoned the final incantation, ending with the invocation, "I command thee to walk!" The echo of these words had scarcely died away when a dazzling white light broke forth from the body, its shrunken form expanded to its natural size and currents of warm blood seemed to animate all its tissues, the dark eyes opened, the lips moved smilingly; then, with a motion so rapid as to be

almost imperceptible to mortal sight, a man, the very
embodiment of physical beauty and strength, sprang to
his feet.

At this marvelous apparition, Doctor Paulus Androcydes bowed his head to the floor, as if in token of adora-
tion.

CHAPTER III.

ATHOTHIS CONVERSES WITH PAULUS ANDROCYDES, AND DIS-
COURSES ON THE DOCTRINE OF METEMPSYCHOSIS—THE
EGYPTIAN REWARDS THE PHYSICIAN FOR HIS VALUABLE
SERVICES.

"RISE, my human benefactor!" said the Egyptian in a clear ringing voice. "Rise and receive any reward you may demand from Athothis, son of Mena." Then the doctor raised his eyes and saw standing over him a form of princely mien, clad in the splendid robes of a magician to the earliest dynasties. This personage extended his hands and lifted the trembling mortal from the floor. "Strange phantom!" gasped Paulus Androcydes, "what art thou?" and the apparition replied, "I am he who but a few moments since resided in your cat Anubis. Oh! mortal, you were a very kind master, and nowhere, during my innumerable transmigrations, have I met better treatment than under your hospitable roof. This is saying much, since I have been a wanderer on the earth for the past sixty-three hundred years. Little did I dream when coming to you as a mere kitten that immortality would so soon be my portion. I had fully expected to transmigrate for at least a million of centuries to come. Imagine my surprise when I first discovered that you were reading the papyrus and uttering my name aloud; fancy my horror when you uncovered the remains of my original habitation; but, above all, judge of my amaze-

ment when I beheld a mortal of the nineteenth century
who had sufficient faith and intelligence to test the experiment formulated in my writings. Oh! what a little
thing it is to perform seeming miracles when one has
faith, for by faith alone man may do things that seem
supernatural."

At these words Doctor Paulus Androcydes marveled
greatly, but plucking up courage, answered, saying: "Can
it be possible that you have wandered over this earth for
sixty-three centuries? Tell me about your many transmigrations, most learned magician!"

Athothis smiled pleasantly, and replied: "I have indeed been a traveler in various forms, in many climes.
I was originally created from the divine essence forty-five
hundred years before the dawn, of what moderns term
Christianity. When first driven out of my primitive
habitation, I transmigrated to the lowest known form of
primordial vegetation. I was then eaten, along with decil-
lions of other transmigrated beings, by a hungry camel.
My evolutions have been so numerous that hundreds of
volumes would not suffice to contain my multiple and
varied experiences. Let me but add that had not my
children taken the precaution to embalm my original
remains I should have continued wandering for ages to
come ; but, following the wisdom of their ancestors, in the
presence of which your modern science is utterly impotent and insignificant, my offspring preserved the
earthly casket of their father, believing in the time-honored doctrine of metempsychosis; for in my day and
generation all mankind had faith in the immortality of
the soul and the final resurrection of the body, and for
this reason embalmed their dead, in the fond hope that at
some time, even in the most distant future, a great power

might restore life to its original habitation. This has chanced to happen to me, and, in the present instance, you were the medium through whom such power was made manifest. How can I ever sufficiently reward you, my mortal friend?"

Doctor Paulus Androcydes bowed his head for a moment as if in deep thought, and answered: "It is true, Athothis, that I have been the medium through whom you have been restored to your great original and man-like form, yet, on reflection, I clearly perceive that all I have done has been through the wisdom set forth in your hieroglyphical scroll. Without the knowledge thus acquired I should have been utterly powerless to render any service; therefore I can not ask, much less expect, a recompense."

Athothis glanced at the doctor approvingly, and said: "You are partially in the right my mortal friend; nevertheless, if you had not had an innate belief in that which was written thousands of years ago, the tests would never have been applied. You may insist that you had no such belief, yet the very fact that you had a lingering doubt implies that you were not altogether devoid of faith."

"As for that," replied the physician, "I fear you deceive yourself, for I have long insisted that ancient authors claimed to know much and really possessed slight knowledge. Strongly imbued with the spirit of scepticism that so extensively pervades scientific circles at the present day, I have always asserted that what was most true in this world was new. I have ever scoffed at its doctrine of immortality and the resurrection of the body, and only yesterday would have laughed to scorn any individual affirming a belief in metempsychosis. As for the Egypt of old, I regarded its ancient religion and customs with curiosity, deeming its people ignorant and superstitious. Regarding embalming, I have agreed with many modern writers that it was only practiced for hygienic purposes; to prevent a contaminated water supply, for instance, as even your benighted countrymen knew that decaying organic matter was dangerous to human life. I suppose you are aware that the most intelligent of latter day Egyptologists insist that the Nile region was destitute of timber, and that the nome dwellers therefore embalmed instead of cremating their dead. As for myself, I am a cremationist."

Athothis laughed merrily as though amused by these observations; then quickly remarked, while his eyes twinkled with a sly gleam of spiritual humor, " I judge you to be an expert at incineration from the promptness and dispatch with which my cat-like covering was consumed in your grate. You speak admiringly of your Egyptologists. Know, my mortal friend, that these modern writers draw largely on their imagination when discoursing of my people. The truth is, that we performed the act of embalming simply to preserve our dead until the resurrection. As for the statement of your latest authorities that it was done on account of a lack of timber in Egypt, that is a ridiculous fallacy. Indeed, we had many other methods for securing intense heat had we been inclined to cremate. One of the most intelligent of your modern writers, Herodotus, came near speaking the truth when he stated that ' the Egyptians mummified their dead in order to prevent them from changing into asses and dogs;' in other words, to keep them from undergoing eternal transmigration. Another distinguished author, Saint Augustine, says that we preserved our dead, by embalming, because we ' believed in the resurrection of the body.' This worthy Saint had really much common sense, a thing seldom found in theologians. I met him about a hundred years ago. He had transmigrated to a gnat-fly, and was busily engaged in annoying a Papal bull by discussing the Manichæan heresy. Another late writer, Mariette Bey, claims that our bodies were embalmed to preserve them until the spirit was purified in purgatory, to be re-united to the body at the resurrection. Perhaps some of the authors on this special subject were inspired with knowledge I do not possess; however, moderns have always been fond of writing ancient history, as it enables them to deal in pleasant fiction and ignore unpleasant facts. It is needless for me to add that I would not be standing in your presence had I not been properly embalmed."

"But the cat was cremated!" exclaimed Paulus Androcydes. "What has become of Anubis?"

"I was Anubis," answered Athothis.

"You surprise me by alluding to Herodotus and Saint Augustine as modern writers," said Paulus Androcydes. "Yet, I am even more astonished to find you familiar with their works since they came into the world centuries after your transmigration from the human form."

"You must certainly admit that these writers were modern when compared to me," responded Athothis, smilingly. "As regards my more recent knowledge of books, that may readily be explained. While I inhabited your cat, for example, I read almost all the tomes on your library shelves. Many of these classics were perused centuries before you were born; for know that, on several occasions, I have been an inmate of immense libraries; thus, I once existed as a pet crane in the

3

Alexandrian library for the space of nineteen years, and during that period carefully studied many thousands of rare documents. When the Alexandrian library was destroyed by burning, A. D. 640, the divine essence was driven out of my crane form, and I entered the body of an infantile bear in what is now known as Chinese Tartary."

"What!" cried Paulus Androcydes, in amazement, "do you wish me to believe that animals read and think? No fact has ever been more clearly demonstrated than that brutes can not reason."

The Egyptian regarded the doctor with an expression betokening pity, and replied : " My mortal friend, you are young yet, and have hardly donned the breech clouts of wisdom ; you have much to learn, and your very remarks indicate the innocence of a prattler. When you have transmigrated for a few thousand years you will commence to acquire a little knowledge of the marvels of this world. Know that all animals, birds, fish, insects, and plants are full of intelligence. Remember that man is the most stupid of created things, until he returns after many ages to his original habitation. As mortals pass through these varied transmigrations they are fully instructed in the mysteries of nature, being taught by actual experience. Man's power of acquiring wisdom becomes intensified in direct proportion to his original inherited ability and inclination for absorbing knowledge. Marvelous power of vision is given to all the lower forms of animal life ; as your cat, I could read through each leaf in every book in your library, even while their covers seemed closed, dark, and unreadable to your ordinary human eyes. This faculty of ever increasing sight will become more apparent to you with each succeeding transmigration."

"I wish I were dead!" exclaimed Paulus Androcydes. "Then could I learn more and more of the mysteries of nature. Oh! what a joyous revelation is this! What infinite delight it will be to wander through the misty ages of the future, when centuries shall be as days and weeks as millions of centuries. How I long to leave my present form of life and plunge into the hereafter. Oh! you have made me happy!"

"Be patient!" remarked Athothis consolingly. "You must live in order to learn; and to live in any form of life is to suffer physical torture. If transmigration has its pleasures, it also has its pains. Oh! mortal man, can you imagine that I, Athothis, would be as happy to-night if transmigration meant eternal bliss. Know that all created things have their joys and sorrows; love and are beloved; are separated by disease or violent deaths. But now, I am the possessor of all secrets and an immortal; restored after many griefs to an infinitude of divine joys, and no longer subject to mental or physical pain. I am truly happy, and can wander through space forever, visiting the sun, moon, and stars, the myriad of planets invisible to human eyes in the vast unfathomless beyond—a thaumaturgist, moving unharmed through earth, air, fire, and water, learning wisdom until the very ages grow gray and Patah creates new worlds of mysteries for solution. This divine bliss comes to all who merit it. It will come to you, if you strive to deserve it by fulfilling well each part assigned in the natural order of creation. Be thankful that you are living to a ripe old age in your present abode, and acquire all the knowledge possible, love deeper, and withal fix your eyes heavenward. Study the stars, and see in their constellations, those brighter intellectual spirits that now sparkle on the bosom of Patah, the Creator of the Universe, the father of all. For it is written in the Book of the Dead, 'Blessed be that life which seeks wisdom through all the revolving ages, for it shall return to Patah, who created it; then shall it become part of the divinity.' "

"You speak of love," said Paulus Androcydes, in evident disdain. "Does that passion still linger in the transmigrating essence?"

"Love is eternal," answered Athothis. "It is the vital spark of the divine essence. Remember that a triad of mystical rules should govern every life; i. e., love Patah, the all-wise, by whom life is given; love every living creature, for every created thing is Patah; love wisdom, for knowledge is power, and Patah alone is all-powerful. He is wisdom. Know, mortal, that as you pass through the various stages of transmigration and are duly initiated into these mysteries, so finally you shall attain your degree of sublime perfection."

Paulus Androcydes trembled violently and extended the ring-finger of his left hand to the Egyptian. As he touched Athothis a strange, thrilling sensation permeated his body; his white, bushy hair seemed to rise on end as if endowed with electric tension, while innumerable sparks flashed before his eyes, and the muscles of his face were so violently twitched that the green glass goggles fell to the floor.

There was a pause of a few seconds, then the kindly voice of Athothis inquired: "In what field of knowledge do you desire to glean information?"

"Enlighten me in regard to medicine; teach me the secrets of the healing art," responded the physician.

Athothis uttered a low sepulchral groan, and then said, in a grave tone: "You shall see modern medical practice as it appears to a physician of an early dynasty. But, in order to become a spirit, it will be necessary to desert your present human habitation for a short space of time. You must become invisible, so that you may accompany me to the sick rooms of your fellow men. You must agree to undergo physical pain and submit to the agony known to mortals as death—which is, after all, but the renewal of life. I will remain with you but a few hours; at the end of which time I will restore your spirit to its primal abiding place, and leave you forever. This is the highest reward I can offer any man. Are you willing to travel with me?"

"Let me suffer the worst of tortures!" cried Paulus Androcydes. "I am willing to submit to any ordeal in order to learn!"

"Brave mortal!" exclaimed Athothis, in a tone of admiration. "I will teach you many curious things; but, first of all, that your spiritual vision may be distinct, you must bow thrice to the east, saying aloud with each inclination of the body, 'Oh, Horus! Divine Horus! Thou son of Ra. I beseech thee let thy light shine on me!' Then, turning, look me in the eye for a single instant. Again incline your head. Then truly you shall learn how rapid is the transition from mortal to spiritual life."

Without a moment's hesitation, and filled with great joy, Doctor Paulus Androcydes bowed to the Orient and repeated the invocation as directed. Turning, he gazed at Athothis, and looking straight into the Egyptian's eyes, he saw flashing in living letters of light the symbols T A O. Before their dazzling splendor the physician bowed his head. At the same instant an electric shock like lightning tore through the mortal's body, and every nerve and tendon seemed cruelly wrenched apart. Doctor Paulus Androcydes uttered a groan of agony, while his earthly casket fell to the floor with a dull heavy thud. Looking down, he saw lying there his former human habitation, its pallid face gazing upward; eyes widely distended, and rapidly glazing; brows bathed in a cold death damp, and muscles slowly contracting with post-mortem rigidity.

"Come!" commanded the voice of Athothis. "Time is precious, and must not be wasted. Let us proceed to investigate modern medicine. Come!"

Doctor Paulus Androcydes found himself floating over the city; and the moonlight was fading away in the west, and the first rosy blush of dawn tinged the eastern sky.

CHAPTER IV.

IN WHICH THE SPIRITS VISIT A MODERN SICK ROOM, AND DOCTOR PAULUS ANDROCYDES IS UNABLE TO MAKE A DIAGNOSIS AFTER SEEING THE DISEASE.

AS the now invisible spirits of Athothis and Paulus Androcydes moved through the air, the latter noticed occasional gleams of light in the windows below.

"Some of our citizens appear to be early risers," remarked the physician; "and yet it can not be more than four o'clock."

"These lights often indicate the presence of sickness," replied Athothis. "Here is an unusually bright ray almost at our feet. Let us enter!" And as he spoke they were wafted over an open transom, borne as lightly as thistle-down on a summer zephyr.

The apartment betokened the presence of persons of luxurious habits and great wealth. The floor was covered with heavy Turkish rugs; the walls hung with satin drapery; the ceiling frescoed in the highest style of art. Delicate lace curtains, as fine as though woven by spiders, drooped from the windows, partially hidden by golden-threaded lambrequins of gorgeous design. The furniture was made of the most expensive hard woods, richly inlaid in arabesque patterns; while the numerous ornaments and pieces of *bric-a-brac* were all in keeping with the artistic taste of the owner

Lying on the bed, in the corner of the room, was a man, moaning and groaning in intense agony, a nurse striving to comfort him; while, bending over the sufferer's bared arm stood a doctor busily engaged in introducing a hypodermic syringe. In the center of the apartment, under the crystal gas-lights, stood two other medical men, wisely stroking their beards and watching their professional *confrere* with apparent interest. Presently, the patient's moans ceased, and a few moments later he fell into a profound doze. Then the three learned doctors retired to an adjoining room, leaving the sick man alone with his servant.

"Behold the wonders of modern medicine!" said Paulus Androcydes. "Notice how calmly the patient rests after the introduction of a little morphine under the skin. He is not in pain now. Ah! the hypodermic is more potent in working wonders than any of the amulets of antiquity."

"What malady does the patient labor under?" queried Athothis.

"I know not, never having examined him," answered Paulus Androcydes.

"Wise man!" remarked Athothis. "Never express an opinion without an examination and a fee! Let us approach the couch and investigate this case."

Gazing at the recumbent form of the sufferer, Paulus Androcydes witnessed an astonishing spectacle—for he perceived, as distinctly as though looking through plate-glass, the entire inner workings of the human organism. He saw the blood circulating within the arteries and veins, and noticed the rapid and excited pulsations of the heart. He watched the lungs contracting and expanding their thousands of air cells. He observed flashes of white electricity, full of latent heat, radiating up and down the spinal column from that great generator of subtile fluid, the brain; while billions of minute, separate and distinct microscopic nervous filaments glowed as distinctly as though under an illuminated lens of the highest imaginable power. He looked at the kidneys, collecting effete and extraneous matter from the circulation, and carrying the minute aqueous particles into the tubules, thence to the ureters, from whence they dropped as amber globules into the bladder. The dark-colored liver seemed to be motionless; and the processes of digestion usually going on in the intestines were quiescent. The stomach was largely distended with a fermenting mass of solids and gases.

As he viewed this wonderful piece of anatomical mechanism in vital action, Doctor Paulus Androcydes experienced a thrill of professional delight, and exclaimed: "Oh! if mortal man possessed this keen spiritual vision, how much more successful would medical practice be!"

"Why this astonishment?" demanded Athothis, in a feigned tone of surprise. "Can it be possible that you, a modern physician, with all your acquirements in anatomy and physiology, are unfamiliar with the workings of the human machine you profess to repair? Can it be that men learned in physic are unacquainted with the first principles of vital movement?"

Paulus Androcydes hesitated a few seconds, then answered: "While it is true that we are not perfectly familiar with the internal workings of the human mechanism, we have nevertheless spent many years of late in a careful study of the anatomical and microscopical construction of the vital organs. We have likewise performed certain experiments in physiology, and made numerous deductions as to the functions of various viscera. As regards the actions of medicinal agents on these organs we have reached the point of perfection, for our wise experimental physiologists and chemists have practiced vivisections on all manner of animals and birds, and thus scientifically determined what effects toxic agents produce on the human system. Why should you suggest, even by inference, that modern physicians are unacquainted with the laws governing vital action? Have we not dissected millions of bodies, and made thousands of autopsies? Ah! Athothis, you know full well that a true knowledge of our noble science was unknown to the ancient Egyptians, who were entirely ignorant of the first principles of anatomy, physiology, and pathology, if we are to believe the statements of modern scientists.'

Athothis indulged in a little ripple of spiritual laughter, and replied : " It is very evident that you never witnessed, until the present moment, the interior machinery of the body in motion. I am fully aware that the anatomists and physiologists of this epoch spend much of their valuable time in dissecting and experimenting on animals. I myself have been a victim of their cruel and senseless practices; for, once, while inhabiting the form of a guinea-pig, a celebrated French *savant* poisoned my system with strychnia, opening the thoracic cavity while my body was yet quivering with life, and, noting the movements of my dying and displaced heart, wrote a learned treatise on the effect of the drug on the cardiac affections of man, basing his conclusions on what he had observed in the differently constructed organism of a guinea-pig. His valuable discoveries were hailed with delight by the medical world. At another period of my

transmigration, while living in the disguise of a pigeon,
a world-renowned scientist in Germany removed sections
of my brain, and afterward published an intensely interesting essay on the localization of the cerebral functions.
Of course, it follows from such experimentations that the
brain construction of birds and mankind is identical.
You indulge in a sneer at the medical knowledge possessed
by the Egyptians; yet, my people were learned in anatomy, physiology, pathology, and therapeutics—for they
constantly opened the bodies of the dead and carefully
studied the removed viscera, thus gaining a perfect understanding of the formation of vital organs, besides becoming very familiar with the pathological changes
wrought by disease. As for anatomy, particularly oste-
ology, the deserts of Egypt were vast charnel-houses, on
which lay exposed the bleached remains of animals, birds,
and men. I, myself, wrote on anatomy, physiology, pathology, and medicine, many centuries before that wise
physician, Hippocrates, was born. Herodotus has truly
stated that the Egyptians hated dissection, and often
stoned our embalmers. This horror of dissection still
exists among moderns, and very few families at the present day will permit post-mortems on relatives. The
world is unchanged in this respect. You are, no doubt,
aware that Pliny admits that the Egyptian kings allowed
autopsies, that physicians might verify their diagnoses;
and that, under many rulers, notably the Ptolomies, anatomy, physiology, and pathology were well understood.
It is even asserted that human beings were opened and
examined while yet alive. The medical men of Egypt
were endowed with clairvoyant power, and were wonderful mind-readers. Come! Doctor Paulus Androcydes,
and acknowledge that, even after viewing the interior of

this patient's body in vital action, you are so utterly ignorant as to the phenomena exhibited, that you are unable to make a correct diagnosis. Seeing the disease, you can not assign a cause for the malady. Come, answer me! What ails this man?"

" 'Tis true, I can not answer immediately," responded the doctor; " I must arouse the patient and subject him to a physical and oral examination. He must relate his symptoms and throw some light on his own case. If he had small-pox, measles, scarlatina, mumps, diphtheria, and many other affections that flesh is heir to, I could make my diagnosis by a simple glance."

" So could any old woman after the disease is fully developed!" retorted Athothis. " But let us suppose that this patient is an infant unable to answer your queries intelligently. How would you determine the nature of the malady in the absence of marked symptoms?"

" Well! well! ah! ah!" stammered Paulus Androcydes, in evident confusion, "I should study the expression of his face, the actions of the body, note the condition of eyes, tongue, pulse, and excretions, auscultate and percuss, inquire into the family history, and then prescribe."

" Without making a diagnosis?" asked Athothis.

" Well! ah! ah! well!" exclaimed the doctor petulantly, "of course I could not clearly determine the nature of the case unless the disease was fully developed, but I would pretend to know all about it, and, in prescribing medicine, should select some remedy that experience has taught me to be good in cases which had exhibited similar symptoms. For instance, the physicians called into the case now under observation prescribed a hypodermic injection of morphine. I know this drug to be a valuable agent for the relief of pain; had I been called to see this sufferer I should have followed precisely the same plan of treatment."

Athothis appeared to be buried in deep thought for a few seconds, and then exclaimed: "So this is your much vaunted modern medical practice; in other words, you are still so-called rational empirics. Know, mortal, that I freely grant that one of the missions of a physician is to relieve pain; nevertheless, before rashly prescribing, you should determine the real cause of distress. In the case before us the diagnosis is perfectly clear. Observe the patient's stomach enormously distended with food, notice this horrible admixture of deviled crabs, stewed oysters, chicken salad, boiled tongue, broiled quail, claret, sherry, champagne, and brandy, completely filling the cavity of the organ. This undigested mass of food is the direct cause of irritation; remove the cause and you relieve the pain. A simple warm water emetic would have been the ancient Egyptian treatment for this case, and the patient would have promptly recovered. As it is, your learned medical men have administered opium in the form of morphine, and have most certainly calmed the sick man's pains. But look! The entire digestive process is checked; the peristaltic action of the intestines has been quieted, and the very efforts that nature makes to relieve itself of a source of irritation are prevented by the action of the remedial agent. In a short time irritation of the stomach will produce sympathetic irritation in other organs; a violent fever might thus be induced, and the patient die. Now, if this man dies, it will be a serious question as to whether the remedy or the disease caused his first transmigration. You speak of morphine as though it were a new medicinal agent for relieving pain and producing sleep; yet, even as a child, I wandered through fields of violet-colored poppy flowers in ancient Egypt, and, in after years, as one of the Court physicians, used the inspissated juice of the plant among the sick and suffering, prescribing it both internally and externally, as the cases seemed to demand. I made mistakes just as you moderns have done; some of my patients went to sleep under the influence of the drug and never woke again; for, as one of your modern writers, Galen, has remarked most wittily: 'The prescription of a medicine is under a physician's control, its effects are not.' But, as this case seems to have awakened your interest, let us enter the adjoining room, where the three wise men of the faculty are now engaged in consultation. It may be that one of the number has some original ideas regarding this malady, its nature, causes, and treatment." Thus speaking, the two spirits entered the consultation chamber.

CHAPTER V.

A MODERN CONSULTATION—AND ATHOTHIS MÁKES A PROG-
NOSIS.

THE three consulting physicians were engaged in earnest conversation. " Who are these men ? " inquired Athothis, and Paulus Androcydes answered : " You see before you Doctors Pillem, Billem, and Killem, all leading practitioners of medicine. These scientists are highly esteemed by the public, and have multitudes of patients among the wealthy and fashionable classes of society. The tall man, sitting at the table examining a clinical thermometer, is Professor Billem, one of the oracles of our faculty ; he lives in finer style than any physician in the city. His brown-stone front is a perfect palace, and the consultation rooms therein are grandly fitted up. There, all the modern instruments of precision are conspicuously displayed and produce a sublime moral effect on his clients. His silver-plated galvanic battery, mounted as handsomely as a concert piano, is always open, and his curious visitors are never weary of casting admiring glances at the mysterious cabalistic symbols on the key-board. A brass-mounted microscope, made in London, regardless of cost, serves as a shining ornament to the expansive bay-window. His walls are adorned with sphygmographic tracings taken directly from the pulses of great statesmen, renowned generals, eminent divines, and the nabobs of the land. Bright colored charts of diseased brains and spinal columns are likewise used for decorative purposes, and entrance the vision of his morbid patrons, who anxiously await their turns for medical consultation. Indeed, Billem's office is a veritable museum to the uninitiated, and the credulous public is impressed with a firm belief that he is one of the most learned men of the age. His library contains over seven thousand volumes in all languages, including Hebrew, Greek, Latin, French, Spanish, Portuguese, German, and English, and he is now studying Russian. He keeps six horses constantly employed in carrying him around to visit patients. He never looks at a client's tongue for less than a ten dollar note, while an extra charge of five dollars is required if he soils his fingers by touching a pulse. His usual compensation for a written diagnosis is fifty dollars, and special consultations, as in this case, at least one hundred. He is greatly envied by his less fortunate professional brothers, who are nevertheless forced to make a virtue of necessity and admit that he has a strong hold on the affections of the community, for in desperate cases people of wealth insist on having the celebrated Billem in consultation, and no fashionable death-bed is complete unless sanctified by his august presence. It is considered the thing in high-toned social circles to have the morning newspapers announce: 'Doctor Billem was consulting physician.' This suffices to convince the public that every thing possible was done to save the deceased; it also serves to protect the regular attending physician from unjust criticism on the part of relatives or jealous outside practitioners, for if Doctor Billem can not save life, who can?"

The smaller individual so wisely stroking his forehead with the index finger of his left hand is another fashionable and extremely erudite physican, Professor Pillem. He likewise has elegantly equipped offices, and is much given to plate-glass mirrors, crystal test tubes, and green retorts ; he includes the laboratory idea in the decoration of his consultation room, and has produced a sensation among business men about town; for Pillem is probably better acquainted with fashionable kidneys than any other doctor in the city, and he is also famed for giving new and expensive remedies ; at present he is running chloride of gold, carbonate of diamond, and acetate of pearl. Pillem has attained great popularity, and does an enormous business; he works four horses constantly.

The cadaveric physican whom we saw administer the hypodermic injection is Professor Killem, an extremely retiring but very learned man. He has acquired a large practice by frequenting a fashionable up-town church; he is of a sweet, gentle, confiding disposition, and never misses attending the funerals of his many patients. Like Billem and Pillem, he is a voluminous author, and his latest work, "A Treatise on the Use of Bananas in Infantile Colic," has had a large sale. However, he has only arrived at the dignity of owning two horses, and boasts of twelve thousand dollars income per annum."

"Enough!" cried Athothis, impatiently. "I care nothing about the business affairs of these gentlemen ; but can see at once from their stylish appearance that they are fashionable doctors. I have noticed, for a hundred years back, that physicians were gaining business sagacity and becoming money-getters, a decided improvement on the philosophical sages of yore, who were happy with a crust of bread and the wick wherewith to burn the midnight oil. I do not wonder that the financial success

4

of these modern professors is greater than their ability to cure disease. A little learning, pompous bearing, much pretense, and plenty of promise are all that is needed at the present day. You speak of the curious collections of instruments and other professional paraphernalia exhibited in the offices of these gentlemen. Know that the mass of humanity ever delighted in the mysterious, and that deception, when cleverly practiced, is usually pleasing. I am fully acquainted with the methods of the professors consulting here; they are merely following in the footsteps of Doctor Forman, Mantaccini, and the Count Cagliostro, all latter-day saints of Paracelsus. I once inhabited the body of a mouse in Cagliostro's house at Saint Petersburg, and saw him receive fees as high as five thousand Louis d'ors. Under the first dynasty, physicians were content to slay afoot; now they slaughter in chariots with horses like Assyrian warriors. But let us listen to the consultation of these erudites." Even as he spoke, Doctor Billem remarked: "It is my opinion, Doctor Killem, that our patient is suffering from neuralgia—lumbo-abdominalis. The direct cause of this outbreak is neurasthenia. I base my diagnosis in this case on the fact that his pains radiate over the region supplied by the ilio-hypogastric nerves. The transversalis muscle is badly affected; the ilio-inguinal nerves likewise involved. But, Pillem, I notice you shake your head in a manner indicating doubt as to the accuracy of my views. Come! give a more rational explanation if you can!"

Doctor Pillem cleared his throat, as though embarrassed, and answered: "Far be it from me to differ with Professor Billem, nor can I expect to discuss with you the delicate points of neurology involved in this exceedingly complicated case; for you are indeed master of your own specialty. There can be no possible doubt but that the ilio-hypogastric and ilio-inguinal nerves are sadly diseased, but I am nevertheless disposed to think that our patient has renal colic, and that the tubules of the papillæ of the kidney, if carefully examined, would reveal the presence of numerous granulated urates. Uric acid infarction is a very common complaint in this city. The frightful agony suffered by our client is due to the passage of a renal calculus from the ureter to the bladder. If I could make microscopical sections of the pyramidal portions of our patient's renal organs, I could show you the characteristic yellowish-red bands extending to the tubules. A full chemical analysis of the urine is necessary in this case, and I shall preserve a specimen for investigation in my laboratory, as I am now preparing a paper for the Philautian Society on this very subject. It is strange, however, that the sick man has not vomited, and this is convincing evidence that the case has numerous complications. If I am permitted to make a suggestion, I should say that the sufferer, in addition to regular hypodermic doses of morphine, should likewise have three hot baths during the twenty-four hours, and also a strong solution of carbonate of lithia. Doctor Killem smiled in a vague, bewildered manner, and, glancing askance at the frowning Professor Billem, said: "I think you are both correct; in other words, we are dealing with a case of lumbo-abdominal neuralgia complicated with renal colic and gastralgia; but I must insist that our patient has gastralgia, since that was my original diagnosis. Have you any suggestions as to treatment, Professor Billem?" The party addressed, glaring angrily at Doctor Pillem, answered wrathfully: "I would amend Pillem's suggestion by adding one-twentieth of a grain of strychnia in combination with five grains of quinine every four hours. Doctor Killem rubbed his hands together as an evidence of delight, and exclaimed : " The very treatment needed! With morphine, hot baths and lithia, strychnia and quinine, our patient must recover. But I will not detain you further, gentlemen! Let us fix the consultation of to-morrow at four o'clock. Is it agreed ? " Professors Billem and Pillem nodded an affirmative to this proposition and retired. It was noticeable, however, that they were out of humor over their disagreement ; nevertheless, a diagnosis had been made ; and what is disease without a diagnosis?

"So this a modern consultation ? " mused Athothis. "Verily the skill of these men surprises me, and their method of arriving at a conclusion is most extraordinary. If medicine is truly a science, as claimed by writers of the present day, one should carefully consider the facts of a given case ; then study the principles based on these facts. In this, as well as in every other patient, a disease can only be determined by a minute examination of the symptoms. Without a true insight as to the significance of morbid signs, no physician can make an accurate diagnosis. This keen perception can not be obtained from books alone, but usually follows observation founded on long experience."

"But these doctors, no doubt, investigated the case before we arrived," remarked Paulus Androcydes. " Know that modern practitioners always carefully examine a patient's tongue and pulse, make numerous queries as to the condition of the secretions and morbid sensations, and likewise carefully auscultate and percuss. In addition, when indicated, they use the microscope, sphygmograph, thermometer, and other scientific instruments of precision."

"Let us concede that these medical scientists have carefully examined the patient, and tested all their instruments of precision," replied Athothis; "nevertheless you must admit that their deductions are entirely wrong, and that they have made three distinct maladies out of a simple case of indigestion. You heard the remarkable proposition of Professor Pillem, that a microscopical section of the pyramids of the kidney would reveal certain morbid changes. This is a mere reflection on death, as the patient must of necessity die in order to verify the statement. Such remarks are common among modern physicians, who seem more prone to study the effects produced by disease rather than to study its treatment. In my time, specialists were more numerous than now; in fact, the ancient Egyptian overdid the business. Yet, my countrymen were not monomaniacs on the subject of their own specialties, like Billem and Pillem, the former of whom diagnoses only diseases of the nervous system, while the latter recognizes no organ save the kidneys. These men judge all maladies by their own standard— like Aretaeus, of Cappadocia, whose knowledge was limited to ague. Mallebranche, who lived centuries after Aretaeus, and appropriated his peculiar ideas, says: 'A new malady makes ravages that surprise the world. If this malady is called the scurvy, all diseases must be called scurvy. The scurvy is new, hence all new diseases must be scurvy. The scurvy is accompanied by dozens of symptoms which are common to other diseases. This makes no difference, for if the patient has any of these symptoms the disease must be scurvy; *ergo*, the sick man must take the treatment laid down for scurvy!'

Now, these remarks may be applied to all specialists, save surgeons and oculists, whose skill is, for the most part, merely mechanical. Look how the last few years have developed specialists in Bright's disease and neurasthenia. It was a time-honored axiom, that there is wisdom in a multitude of counselors. But this rule only works confusion when applied to modern medical men."

"You are too severe," said Paulus Androcydes, in an expostulating voice. "You neither appear to value the minute knowledge of a special subject acquired by some physicians, nor do you seem to consider their consultations of much value. Are you not aware that no one man can master the immense field occupied by modern medicine, nor become expert in all branches of our noble science? Is it not better to become perfect in one disease rather than imperfect in all? I suppose you will claim that Egypt, Greece, and Rome had better physicians than the present age; and, because many of your learned men walked afoot, lived on dry crusts, and even wanted for the wick wherewith to burn the midnight oil, they were therefore more skillful than moderns."

"You are indulging in sarcasm," responded Athothis, in a tone of amusement. "You evidently do not comprehend my remarks. Believe me, I do not undervalue a special knowledge on medical subjects, and fully agree with you that no mortal man can compass the entire domain of medical wisdom, neither acquire a perfect understanding of every branch of the healing art. But the body is such a complicated piece of mechanism, and the manifestations of disease so numerous, that a general knowledge of the whole organism, even though very imperfect, is better than the special skill just manifested in this consultation. Billem and Pillem are true specimens of the narrow-minded specialists of this age. In ancient Egypt we exposed our patients in the market-places and other public resorts, in order that any wise passer-by might examine the case, and express an opinion; but only one doctor treated the disease."

"That was rank quackery!" cried Paulus Androcydes, indignantly. "For certainly no definite diagnosis could be made when the number of consultants was so enormous. And it is certain that the sick must have died then, even as now, from errors in diagnosis, and therefore maltreatment."

"Greece and Rome practiced empiricism," remarked Athothis, laughingly. "The Romans once survived six hundred years without a recognized faculty or medical school; while such distinguished citizens as Cato, for example, practiced medicine without a diploma. Slaves were taught how to prescribe by their masters, and became very expert in applying remedies. Cabbage was a famous medicinal agent in those days, and is said to have cured more persons than it killed. These ancient peoples discovered that aloes and colocynth were purgatives. There were likewise wise lawyers who formulated rules and regulations on sanitation; there were engineers who fully appreciated the value of an uncontaminated water supply and good drainage, and constructed aqueducts and well-ventilated sewers never equaled by moderns; there were epicures who were also philanthropists, and instructed the people in the real art of cookery; there were—"

"Hold!" exclaimed Paulus Androcydes. "Yet, people died?"

"True," answered Athothis, "men and women died then, as now. Yet, withal, medicine was more honored

than at the present day. For it was even then written
that, 'God created the physician and physic. He hath
given wisdom to man and to him that healeth man.'
Even Hippocrates acknowledged that medicine was the
invention of the divinity. Did not Cicero contend that
the practice of the healing art was sacred? Ah! these
ancients had a higher appreciation of medical wisdom
than your moderns, for they erected beautiful temples to
the founders of the profession, to Osiris and Isis, to
Apollo and Minerva. You scoff at the medical knowledge of antiquity, yet seek to give a poor imitation of
its methods. You deride the learned magi of the Orient,
and believe that the scientists of this age possess all the
wisdom of the past and present. We have just witnessed
the learned consultation of Doctors Billem, Pillem, and
Killem, perfect types of the specialists of the day; think
you that their attainments are greater than those of the
fathers of medicine? Yet, you endeavor to impress the
modern public with the idea that all real knowledge of
the healing art is new, that the accumulated erudition
of the past is nothing. Has not Celsus truthfully claimed
that 'medicine and mankind are coeval.' Has not Pliny
written that 'while some nations have existed without
doctors, none ever lived without physic'? It is an easy
matter to assert that ancient physicians killed millions
of patients through ignorance. Can you deny that they
may not have healed an equal number? But, see!
Killem is standing in the center of the room preparing
another hypodermic of morphia for his suffering client.
And you remarked that this eminent practitioner was a
strict member of an orthodox church; nevertheless, he
is now preparing to violate, though ignorant of the fact,
the sixth commandment."

"What!" cried Paulus Androcydes, in amazement. "Can it be that the patient will die? Indigestion rarely kills."

"But medicine often does," replied Athothis, dryly. "My prognosis is, crape on the front door-knob in twenty-four hours. For, when three consulting physicians diagnose as many different diseases, and prescribe morphia, hot baths, lithia, strychnia, and quinine, poor humanity must needs order a shroud and prepare for the grave."

"Let me stay this cruel work!" exclaimed Paulus Androcydes, excitedly, darting forward and endeavoring to tear the instrument from Doctor Killem's hands.

Whereat, Athothis laughed at the impotence of the spiritual attempt, and remarked: "Come! no violence, if you please. Recollect that you are powerless at present. Besides, the patient's fate is already sealed, and his name is inscribed on the scroll of the silent passers away, on the records of Osiris. Look! Doctor Killem has already inserted another dose of his poison."

Even as he made this remark, the deadly needle was withdrawn from the sick man's arm, and he calmly slept on, apparently unmindful of the operation.

"He dreams sweet dreams of his youth and loving mother," continued the Egyptian. "Away!"

The first beams of glorious sunlight were peeping in at the windows, and again the spirits gently floated through the ambient ether.

5

CHAPTER VI.

ATHOTHIS AND PAULUS ANDROCYDES MEET A MODERN
PHYSICIAN OF A RARE OLD TYPE.

THE sun had now risen above the horizon and its warm cheerful radiance was fast dissipating the last vapory atoms of foggy mist. On the western outskirts of the city, where the houses sloped up the hill-sides in terraces one above the other, thousands of windows reflected the golden rays of the eastern sky. On the highlands, surrounding the suburban portion of the town, the forests and meadows had donned the full virginal robes of spring. The air was redolent with the odor of violets, apple blossoms, and honeysuckles, while the twittering and warbling of numerous feathered songsters filled the heavens with charming melody.

"What a delightful morning! What a superb prospect!" exclaimed Paulus Androcydes in a tone of ecstasy, as he viewed with intense admiration the grand panorama outstretched below.

"'T is the annual awakening of Seb from his winter's nap," remarked Athothis, "and the earth is never so happy as when attired in a new suit of green, white, and red. But here is an open garret lattice, and I hear moans; let us enter." And, therewith, the spirits drifted into a shabby old tenement house, into a dingy-looking room. This dwelling-place denoted the presence of abject poverty, the furniture consisting of three broken-down chairs and an old dry goods box that served at once for a bureau and wash-stand, as was evident from the fact that the open lower portion contained a few neatly-folded bundles of patched clothing, while the top was adorned by a battered tin wash-basin and a cracked china pitcher. There was no carpet on the floor, which was, however, clean and white. The walls were covered by dozens of colored pictures from cheap illustrated periodicals. Overhead was a rough-plastered ceiling, the principal decoration of which was a large crack that permitted a view of the blue sky above.

On a rickety and scantily-covered bed lay the emaciated shadow of what had once been a vigorous man. Standing at the side of the couch, with her cool hand on the feverish sufferer's brow, was a thin, wan woman, whose faded calico dress revealed the outlines of an almost perfect form; her face was still beautiful, though pinched by hunger and sorrow, yet it lighted up with a pleasant smile as the sick man opened his eyes in response to her magnetic touch. Stooping over she kissed his pale forehead, as he moaned in a low, weak voice: "Another day of misery. Oh! Maggie, this is too hard! Here I have been, a month to-day, lying helpless on my back, while you and baby are starving!" She kissed him again, and patted him affectionately on the head; but the patient, gently pushing his wife aside, raised up in the bed and broke out in a violent fit of coughing. This spasmodic action lasted for several moments, growing more and more violent, until the larger veins in the sufferer's temples stood out like whip-cords, while his face grew purple from asphyxia; then,.with a mighty physical effort, he coughed up and expectorated several mouthfuls of mucus, and, with a sigh of relief, fell back on the pillow utterly exhausted. While this was occurring, a puny three-year old child sat on the floor nursing a shabby rag doll, her baby eyes filled with tears of sympathy and infantile wonder. Presently the woman, in a coy, half-hesitating manner, remarked: "Charley, I went after a doctor this morning; you must neglect yourself no longer. I am so afraid that this cough may affect your lungs." The sick man turned his head, and said in a petulant, chiding voice: "Why did you do this, Maggie? You know we have no money to buy bread, much less medicine; besides, the doctor will expect his fee." "Yes! but I have obtained a little money," answered the woman with sudden eagerness. "I went to the pawnbroker's this morning, and he advanced three dollars on my—" Here her voice faltered, and she raised a coarse cotton apron to her eyes. "Why!" exclaimed the husband, in a tone of surprise and bitterness, "I thought we had nothing left valuable enough to pawn or sell." "'Twas my wedding ring," murmured the wife, bursting into tears. "Oh! Maggie, how could you?" groaned the man, pulling the woman's head against his breast, and fondly caressing her. "My cup of sorrow is now filled to overflowing."

"This is too much!" cried Paulus Androcydes, dropping his spiritual hand in a vain search for a material pocket-book. At this instant a loud knock was heard at the door, and the woman, hurriedly wiping her eyes, arose and lifted the catch.

A heavy-set man, with round bullet-like head and closely-cropped black whiskers, made his entrance, cap in hand, his dark eyes fairly sparkling as he cast a quick, keen glance around the room. This individual was attired in a threadbare suit of clothing, cut in the fashion of ten years previous. Without a word of salutation, the newcomer picked up one of the broken chairs, and placing it at the patient's bedside, opened a conversation without further ceremony.

"That's old Doctor Soother," remarked Paulus Androcydes, in a voice of commingled pity and derision.

"Who is this Soother?" demanded Athothis, his grim, spiritual face relaxing into a pleasant smile.

"Oh! he's a doctor about town, a rough old professional growler—what we moderns term a crank," replied Paulus Androcydes disdainfully. "He is an old bachelor who has practiced about thirty years and scarcely earns his salt. Look at his face and hands! They certainly are not on familiar terms with soap and water. Do you not detect the odor of stale tobacco smoke exhaled from his coat? A delicate medical attendant, forsooth, for a sick person with refined olfactories. No wonder such a shabbily-dressed and ill-mannered man as Soother should fail in fashionable practice. He will never attain greater eminence than tenement house doctor."

"Come! come!" interrupted Athothis, angrily, "I can judge of his personal appearance myself, and only desire to know of his professional worth; for, believe me, under the first dynasties, a man's clothing and personal habits were no gauges of mental ability. Is Soother a physician of intelligence?"

"I know not," responded Paulus Androcydes, with a sneer. "'Tis a matter on which I am not informed, but it is said his office is filled with grimy old books and morbid specimens. If Soother possesses any extensive medical knowledge he certainly hides his light under a bushel, since he has never been known to air his opinions in the Philautian Medical Society, and seems to studiously avoid discussing professional questions with other physicians. He does not contribute to journals on physic, and is, therefore, no scientist."

"In other words, because this man is modest and retiring, and makes no long-winded orations before those mutual admiration medical societies, he is ignored," said Athothis; "and his careless dress and habits likewise create professional prejudice against him. Know that many of the wisest philosophers and sages were extremely careless as regards dress. Why, all the cynics, including Diogenes, had a contempt for personal appearance, and went unwashed."

"Such men are public nuisances," replied Paulus Androcydes. "Diogenes would have been sent to prison for vagrancy in these days of refinement; for ancient history states that he was a filthy old man in all his habits. Remember the proverb, 'Cleanliness is next to godliness.'"

"But," interposed Athothis, "transmigration cures many original natural defects, and, speaking of Diogenes, reminds me of the fact that I met him in Portugal about two hundred years ago; he was inhabiting the body of a gorgeous butterfly, and was sipping the nectar from a rose, when he was rudely gobbled up and swallowed by Antisthenes, who was strutting around in the brilliant plumage of a peacock. As for cleanliness and godliness, they frequently exist apart, and you must admit that one of your orthodox disciples, Saint John, never changed his clothing, and neglected ablution, although fond of baptizing others, while good Saint Hilarion could never be induced to even wash his undershirt. Ah! no, dirt, genius, and true piety often go hand in hand. But look! Doctor Soother is questioning the patient."

Paulus Androcydes smiled contemptuously, and responded: "Any half-witted physician can make a diagnosis in this case by merely looking at the sick man. His emaciation, hectic, and cough at once indicate him to be in the last stages of consumption."

"Softly! softly!" cautioned Athothis. "Be careful lest you fall into error again! Let us look into the case before rendering a rash decision."

Doctor Soother was now writing down notes in a large memorandum book, inscribing the patient's answers to numerous queries. Among the many questions asked were those relative to the duration of the illness, the manifest primary symptoms of the malady, the medical treatment followed, previous habits of the individual, occupation and family history, with many other details that sadly wearied the spiritual patience of Paulus Androcydes. Finally, Doctor Soother took a common stethoscope; then, alternately percussing and auscultating the sick man's chest, he noted the patient's temperature with a clinical thermometer, observed the tongue, felt the pulse, and so concluded his examination.

From the conversation between physician and client, the spirits learned that the man had been ill for about a month, had contracted a severe cold, accompanied by fever, sense of oppression in the chest, cough and considerable expectoration at times; had taken no drugs save patent medicines prescribed by a neighboring chemist. His habits of life had been extremely correct; he had been raised in comparative luxury; there was no marked hereditary taint in his family. In early life he lived on a farm; afterward became a banker in a village, where he had lost all his money in unfortunate speculations. Drifting with his family to the great city, he had been

unable to obtain any employment, and having no wealthy
relatives nor friends, and sick with disease and discour-
agement, he had finally taken to his bed.

"Gaze at Soother's wonderful note book!" remarked
Paulus Androcydes, looking over the doctor's shoulder
as he spoke. "Behold the memorandum! 'Case 1086.
Bronchitis simulating phthisis. Direct cause, exposure
and bad nutrition.' Did you ever hear such a stupid
opinion? I now perceive that Doctor Soother is an
ignoramus and can not detect consumption from bronchitis. I repeat what I said before that the patient is in
the last stages of — "

"Starvation!" cried Athothis, finishing the sentence.
"This Doctor Soother is perfectly correct in his diagnosis,
while you are entirely wrong. Cast your spiritual vision
and closely scan the condition of the sick man's respira-
tory organs. You will at once perceive the extent of the
difficulty, and know that the affection is perfectly amenable to treatment. I have the greatest curiosity to see
what the clear-headed Soother will prescribe."

"Well! well! can it be possible that a man of my
vast clinical experience is again mistaken?" groaned
Paulus Androcydes, in an abashed and mortified voice;
then added, with a sigh: "Now is the time to give syrup
of senega and carbonate of ammonia in order to promote
expectoration." But, even as he muttered these words,
Doctor Soother drew from his pocket a ragged old wallet,
tied around with a piece of dirty tape, and taking therefrom a small wad of greasy-looking bank notes delib-
erately counted out ten one dollar bills and tendered the
money to the patient's wife, who, drawing back with an
air of wounded dignity, declined the generous proffer.
At this refusal to accept money, Doctor Soother seemed

to grow angry, for he exclaimed: "Madam, do you desire to see your husband restored to health?" And the poor wife, clasping her hands nervously, replied: "I would lay down my life for him!" Whereat, the physician, with even more vehemence, retorted: "Of course you would, like any other fool woman!" then added, in a commanding voice, still extending the bank notes: "Here! take this prescription immediately. Go to the grocer on the opposite corner. Buy a soup bone, vegetables, bread, coffee, tea, butter, sugar, and milk! Eat! and make your husband and child eat, for it's very evident you are all starving. Do what I bid, madam, and your husband will recover. His life is now in your hands."

The woman accepted the money, but the sick man, in a chiding way, exclaimed: "Doctor, this is not right, I can never repay you, for I shall never be able to rise from this bed again." "Nonsense!" answered the doctor, "I will have you all right in another month, and, in the meantime, I will hunt you up some work so that you may repay me the money necessary for your support until such a time as you recover." Then, turning to the woman, he remarked: "The sooner you make soup for this man the better, for he needs soup, good nutritious soup! Put in plenty of vegetables, especially onions; don't forget to buy onions! Do you hear? Onions! I will bring some medicine this evening, but for the present, soup. Do you understand? Soup with onions!" And, rushing to the door, Doctor Soother disappeared; and as his heavy and rapid footsteps echoed along the tenement house stairs, and finally were lost in the distance, two pairs of lips murmured: "God bless him!"

"That was an old time type of a doctor," said Atho-

this, in tones of sincere admiration. " Soother is humanity, charity, and medicine combined."

" He is an old crank ! " cried Paulus Androcydes.

" He is a true philanthropist ! " replied Athothis.

" The very idea of giving a sick man onion soup ! " exclaimed Paulus Androcydes, in accents of disgust. " Soups
may be proper in this case, but, I decidedly object to the
onion."

" Doctor Soother is really a skilled physician, said
Athothis, musingly, " and his views of this case are perfectly correct.   I read his mind as he carefully examined
the patient's symptoms and made his deductions ; and I
felt a sympathy for the doctor when he came to prescribe
and was obliged to deplete his own lean pocket-book in
order to fatten up the sick man.   How different is the
fate of this client and the one now being treated by Billem, Pillem, and Killem.   In the latter case the attending
physicians know an immense estate will be left, and that
the grateful heirs will not quibble over a large fee ; but
this pauper patient has secured the services of a
doctor who intends to use the best possible medical
judgment for the mere love of healing.   Blessed are the
poor, for they shall receive the first fruits of medical
wisdom, while the rich must suffer from professional
ignorance and avarice.   Doctors Billem, Pillem, and
Killem are mere mushrooms, living off the manure heap
of knowledge ; while this plain old crank, as you term
him, is a gentleman of intelligence and withal has a
heart.   Yet I fear that Soother's practice in the future
as in the past, will be limited to the poorer classes from a
sheer love for doing good.   He will never allow his attention to be attracted from his professional studies by
such trivial matters as soap and water, nor will he have

the leisure time necessary for personal adornment; hence he will not merit the patronage of the wealthy and refined. He will never boast of the remarkable knowledge of medicine he possesses, nor drive four horses, and will therefore remain unknown to most of his professional brothers. When he passes from his present mortal habitation no monument will be raised over his remains; but his epitaph will be inscribed on the tablets of each grateful patient's memory. But, in all his transmigrations, he will be fully initiated in nature's most hidden secrets, and shall receive a final reward at the hands of the Grand Master. I am happy to have seen this rare old type of doctor, and doubt not that there may be a few others like him. Soother has led me to overcome one prejudice which has clung to me during all my varied changes."

"What may that prejudice be?" asked Paulus Androcydes, in eager curiosity.

"Onions!" responded Athothis; "for, in my day and generation, we Nile dwellers were taught that the onion was a sacred plant, the divine symbol of planetary revolutions, the renewal of the ages. Yet this impious doctor of the nineteenth century has prescribed it for the renewal of a pauper's health; and, I foresee that the effect of the plant will be good. Ah! even we immortals at last learn to cast prejudices aside. But come! let us be going." And again the spirits were whisked out into space.

CHAPTER VII.

DOCTOR PAULUS ANDROCYDES ADMITS THAT MODERN MED-
ICINE IS A MERE TRADE AND HATH ITS TRICKS.

" ORTUNE, the fickle goddess, never bestows her gifts so blindly and capriciously as in the medical profession," mused Paulus Androcydes, as he rested with Athothis in mid-air for the moment. " The lives of most doctors are full of tribulations, and where one practitioner attains eminence ten thousand fail." " True," responded Athothis; " for the simple reason that your modern public too often extends its patronage to the unworthy and places confidence in those who can lay no honest claim to the degree of doctor. At the present day, fashion and accident lead to celebrity. Some wealthy bell-wether draws the social flock, while society's lamb-kins and the common herd bah the praises of the ignorant, and make a shepherd of the wolf. Notoriety is esteemed the sign of genius, while obscurity is the certain indication of a fool. Arrogance grows rich; modesty starves. Mediocrity rides in a chariot, while true worth travels afoot. 'Tis the age of Brass! Do you ride or walk, doctor?"

"I ride!" answered Paulus Androcydes, proudly and with defiance; "for remember, my Egyptian friend, that this is a practical age. To merit success is one thing, to secure it another. The acquirement of public confidence at the present time requires the most delicate circumspection and tact. Competition is so keen that one must be very politic, and the majority of thriving practitioners are skilled diplomats. We must cater to all of society's whims and prejudices, at the same moment concealing our own individualities by constant dissimulation. We must appear to the public that which we are not; in other words, assume to know all of which we are ignorant in order to be accused of wisdom."

"In other words, you are hypocrites!" exclaimed Athothis, indignantly; "so that you may receive a pecuniary reward at the hands of an equally intelligent public. I am glad to see that you are candid enough to admit that great medical success among moderns, in the vast majority of instances, implies the practice of cunning and trickery, and that the noble art of healing is sunk to the level of trade?"

"Precisely!" answered Paulus Androcydes, in a semi-apologetic tone. "The modern commercial world judges all professional men by its own standard, and considers pecuniary success the only real test of ability. When a a physician secures a large practice, for instance, he attains the same degree of eminence as our established mercantile house, and can defy the competition of less astute business rivals; for, following their ordinary commercial instincts, the great majority of people go to the shop that appears to attract the most customers, as the established reputation of such a firm seems to afford extra inducements. As for the moral and intellectual worth of the proprietor they care naught."

"They are not as wise as one of the recent Popes," quoth Athothis, smilingly, "who was ever careful in the choice of his physician. This Pope, whose love for truth and honesty was only equaled by his affection for Saint Peter, had the misfortune to lose an old medical attendant, and announced his desire for a new doctor. Dozens of celebrated practitioners applied for the high honor, and His Holiness invariably asked each aspiring candidate, "How many patients have you killed?" and the universal reply was, "I do not kill; my practice is to cure," and were promptly shown the door. Finally, one bright Summer's morning, a ragged, shabby-looking fellow craved an audience, and in response to the Pope's usual query answered, "*Tot quot.*" Whereupon his holiness embraced the obscure individual, saying: "Thou art my choice ; for verily thy truthfulness begets faith, and without faith one can not be saved."

"*Si non e vero e ben trovato !*" remarked Paulus Androcydes, sarcastically. "I suppose that you have met this wise old Pope in some of your numerous transmigrations ?"

"You are wrong," answered Athothis, softly. "Such rare wisdom reaped its just reward ; for His Holiness was spiritually translated and never suffered the pains and tortures of transmigration. His knowledge of human nature, especially of doctors, made him infallible. He has been canonized above."

"Behold a modern physician driving under us now !" cried Paulus Androcydes. "Look at his trim figure attired in the faultless costume of the period ; view his shining silk hat and exquisitely fitting boots ; note his lemon-colored kid gloves and dainty button-hole bouquet ; observe the graceful nonchalance with which he leans back on the satin-covered cushions of his elegant coupe. He is absorbing wisdom from the book he so eagerly peruses. See how the people gaze in admiration as the equipage rolls past and mentally exclaim: "What a learned and swell young man is Doctor Beaumonde! He studies medicine even while driving to visit his patients!"

"Yes!" responded Athothis, laughing in high glee. "He is reading indeed; but cast your spiritual eyes on the title-page of the volume, and behold, 'The Crushed Heart, a Romance of Cardiac Affection.'"

"You are right!" exclaimed Paulus Androcydes, smilingly. "Yet, Doctor Beaumonde enjoys a large practice among the fashionable fair sex; and no social gathering is complete without his presence. He is the cynosure of all eyes as he enters a drawing-room. His manners are simply perfect, and polite society fairly worships the young doctor. His, is the most extravagant and elaborate wardrobe in the city. No one knows this better than his tailor, who is obliged to take out his bill in professional services. Doctor Beaumonde is now on his way to call on one of his fair lady clients, who is suffering from that fashionable malady known as neurasthenic malaria. She contracted this affection at the last Charity Ball, the doctor being her medical attendant at the time. His carriage will linger in front of her palatial mansion for an hour, until the curious and inquisitive neighbors are duly impressed with the serious nature of the case; while within Doctor Beaumonde will discourse on the last new figure in the German, the physical benefits of the waltz, champagne as a sovereign remedy for sea sickness, clubs and bars as cures for masculine dyspepsia; then he will look at his patient's tongue, feel her pulse ever so tenderly, indite a prescription, and take his leave. The lady's husband, in the meanwhile, will be worrying over his ledger down town, endeavoring to conjure up some plan for increasing his income, for he has many large bills to pay, among the least of which is

not that of his fashionable physician. Doctor Beaumonde has numerous clients of this class to visit, and is
very happy, basking in the sunshine of Fortune."

"You are using your spiritual vision expertly," remarked Athothis, approvingly. "But here comes another
stylish medical vehicle, with coachman and livery. I
observe that its occupant is a severe, drowsy-looking
individual, who is either deeply buried in meditation or
half asleep. He must have acquired his professional
poise by hard study and many rehearsals in front of a
glass. He wishes to appear learned and weary at the
same time, so that the admiring public may say : ' Look
at the wise old doctor ; he has broken down his health
from overwork and devotion to suffering humanity. Ah!
he needs our support and sympathy.' "

"You have read him correctly," said Paulus Androcydes ; for that is the eminent Doctor Toiler, one of the
professors in the Medical College of Utopia. Toiler has
an enormous practice ; and every afternoon, from two to
five, prescribes for patients by the score. He is a
formualist, and uses but four remedies ; *i. e.*, castor oil,
calomel, morphine, and quinine. He has no time to
write out formulæ in full, and so numbers them recipes
1, 2, 3, 4. This enables the pharmacist, as he needs but
few medicines, to buy his stock at wholesale ; no mistakes are made in compounding, and the druggist has
grown wealthy. Happy the apothecary who hath such a
patron !

"Toiler's business is principally among old and young
married women. He is the medical high priest to whom
most fashionable wives have confessed the shortcomings
of husbands, the misfortunes of sons, the conjugal infe-
licity of daughters. His bosom is a closet wherein are

concealed the family skeletons of a hundred households; and, to his credit be it said, he sacredly guards the confidences of his clients. Yet, more than one person will breathe easier when Toiler passes away, 'for dead men tell no tales.' He is feared as well as trusted, and his bills are never disputed by the cowardly heads of families. It is needless to say that Toiler is rich and respected, because he enforces respect; for his word is law. When called in consultation with other practitioners, he is coldly patronizing, and never deigns to discuss the medical features of a case; thus, his superiors in wisdom are obliged to defer to his opinions without question. It is noticeable, moreover, that those forced to call him in consultation usually lose the confidence of their clients, who ever after retain Toiler's valuable services. His judgment of other practitioners is rather critical, and he is apt to remark: 'Yes, he has talent, and will learn to prescribe as he grows older,' or 'If he had more experience, the patient might have recovered.' He delivers popular lectures for the benefit of charities, and reprints his remarks for gratuitous distribution among the laity. He is the author of a number of works having a paying circulation; as, for instance, 'Hints to Young Mothers,' 'The Care of the Aged,' 'Humanity in the Sick Room,' 'Diet of Infancy,' 'Beef Tea and How to Make It.' Toiler is now on his way to visit a fashionable old dame, the widow of a wealthy banker, who is confined to bed from an attack of pleurisy, due to a cold contracted from wearing a low-necked dress in a stage box at the opera. She would insist on assuming this Eve-like costume, because encouraged by her son-in-law, who is now, of course, greatly alarmed lest his wife's mother may die

6

and leave him a million dollars to manage. Toiler's carriage will stop at the widow's mansion for only a few moments, as the doctor wastes no time on long calls. He will prescribe numbers 1, 2, 3, 4, as the case may seem to indicate, and retire as rapidly as he came."

"Here comes another doctor's chariot!" cried Athothis. "What a gorgeous turnout! 'T is a superb livery, and the gold-mounted harness fairly glitters in the sun; but see the vacant-looking stare of the occupant as he steadfastly gazes at the gilt buttons on his driver's coat tail. He looks like a German theological student, with his snow-white choker, long black suit, and plain glass spectacles. His head is all out of proportion to his feet, which are large; and yet methinks his brow seems overcast by a sickly gleam of intelligence. He has a small black patent-leather case on the cushion beside him. Perhaps it holds instruments, and he is some young rising surgeon!"

"It is Doctor Moonshine," said Paulus Androcydes. "He is one of our leading homeopathic practitioners; and permit me to say that he deserves great credit for the manner in which he has pushed himself to the front. Ten years ago he was a stable boy, and picked up a smattering of veterinary medicine from giving boluses and enemas to horses. But, coming to the conclusion, like numerous other bright minds of the age, that he had talent of a high order, he entered the infinitesimal department of Humbug University, and graduated in six months, his thesis on "The Quadrillioneth of a Grain of *Mephitis Americana* in Flatulence" attracting widespread attention from the advocates of the sugar-pellet school. Really the fellow is utterly ignorant of anatomy, physiology, and pathology, and misspells the names of

ordinary remedies. Yet he has the confidence and patronage of hundreds of otherwise intelligent people."

"I am glad to see one genuine disciple of Hahnemann,"
quoth Athothis, "for such practitioners are rare. If your
statements regarding his ignorance are true, he is nevertheless an honest man, for know that the founder of the
system he follows was one of the first to teach that a
knowledge of anatomy, physiology, and pathology was
not needed to make a good doctor, for Hahnemann de-
claims against those physicians who base their treatment
on conclusions derived from such branches of knowledge;
ergo, ignorance on the subjects mentioned implies a true
insight into the system of the author of the Organon.
Besides, your true practitioner of homeopathy need never
vex his mind for a diagnosis. He should not say, for
instance, that a child has scarlet fever, measles, whoop-
ing-cough or diphtheria; for the father of Moonshine's
system distinctly maintains that any expression denoting
a collection of symptoms is not applicable to disease, and
should be omitted in the discussion of medicine, which
merely consists of therapeutics. As all disorders of mankind, except one, are the result of a deadly psoric miasm,
which evidences itself in a multitude of symptoms, it is
an easy matter to understand what disease really is. As
for your true homeopathic treatment it can do no harm
if it doth no good. Mothers of families can safely prescribe for the symptoms of this psoric miasm by following
simple text-books, and as the remedies are innocent little
pellets the school must be very popular. Why people
who profess to understand this system of medicine employ any doctor is one of the mysteries of the century."

"But we must observe the formalities of life," said
Paulus Androcydes. "No sick bed is complete without

a doctor, and the time-honored custom has been to make the physician prescribe."

" Under these circumstances, such men as Moonshine must thrive," answered Athothis; " and so long as the world is pleased to employ his scientific services, and he only continues to prescribe grains of sugar, no great harm is done.

" Here comes another two-horse chariot," interrupted Paulus Androcydes, " and lolling within is a smiling, sweet-faced young man, who, judging from his self-satisfied appearance, is at peace with his own conscience and all mankind. Notice the manner in which he puckers up his lips! Listen! he is whistling the Dead March, from Saul."

" What is that object lying on the carriage seat?" inquired Athothis. " Can it be that he is driving around with a child's coffin?"

Paulus Androcydes indulged in a spiritual smile, and answered : " The object you notice is a violin case and only contains the remains of a Stradivarius. This is young Doctor Symphony, a man of infinite genius and remarkable intellect, whose soul is wrapped up in a deep contemplation of music and medicine. Doctor Symphony has an enormous practice among musically inclined people, and is much employed by fathers who have marriageable daughters and believe with Erasmus '*Musicam docet amor et poesin*.' He is now on his way to visit a hysterical woman, who is devoted to the piano, and practices, much to the annoyance of the neighbors. Presently Symphony will accompany the lady in a duet; thus musical instruction is combined with medicine, and the young woman's father will ask for no discount on the bill. But permit me to assure you that Symphony is really a gentleman of no mean medical ability, and hath much culture, for he reads many interesting papers before the Philautian Medical Society, among which may be mentioned: 'The Musical Qualities of the Umbilical Chord,' 'Notes on the Sphincter,' 'Essay on the Drum of the Ear,' 'Maladies of the Digestive Organs,' etc. Yes, Symphony is a man of genius, and is rapidly accumulating a fortune."

"Enough!" cried Athothis. "Let me hear no more or you will next convince me that modern medicine is the science of deceiving the public. So you acknowledge that success in the healing art requires neither wisdom nor honesty?"

"I admit that medicine, like all other trades, hath its tricks," replied Paulus Androcydes. "But, see that gathering of doctors' carriages opposite the brown-stone front below! Let us descend and enter, as some important operation is about to be performed. Come!" So saying, the two spirits dropped down a high chimney, alighting in the parlor of a wealthy merchant.

CHAPTER VIII.

THE SPIRITS WITNESS AN ANCIENT SURGICAL OPERATION—
AND ATHOTHIS PRAISES JEWISH DOCTORS, MUCH TO THE
DISGUST OF PAULUS ANDROCYDES.

THE parlor was furnished in the highest style of oriental magnificence, and was half filled with swarthy men, whose features indicated a Semitic extraction.

Seated on a divan, in the full light of the window, was a patriarchal father of Israel, whose bronzed face, prominent nose, and dark careworn eyes were intently bent over the form of an infant which lay on a pillow in his lap. Kneeling on a cushion in front of this patriarch was another venerable man, whose snow-white hair and long flowing silvery beard evidenced a ripe old age.

Gathered around, and quietly watching the skillful manipulations of the operator, were a number of guests, including several physicians.

"The Jewish faculty seem to be enjoying itself this morning," remarked Paulus Androcydes, in a sneering tone. "With the natural timidity of their race they are mere lookers on in surgery and leave even this simple operation to a non-professional. What a superstitious and barbarous custom is this !"

"Behold the wisdom of this ancient people !" said Athothis. "They continue to practice the useful hygienic measures handed down to them by the Egyptians."
"I have always been taught that circumcision originated

with the Jews, and was first practiced by Abraham nineteen hundred and forty-one years before the establishment of Christianity!" replied Paulus Androcydes.

Athothis smiled and answered: "You hold to the usual erroneous ideas of moderns."

"Yet I based my belief on the Bible, the Book of Prophets, and the Talmud," retorted Paulus Androcydes, "and surely your chronology does not antedate the Book of Genesis!"

"I was born centuries before Abraham," responded Athothis with dignity. "The operation of circumcision is as old as Egypt, for does not our most ancient papyrus speak of the blood that fell from the phallus of the Sun-god when he had finished cutting himself. Go back to the beginning of time, when Isis wandered disconsolate in search of her beloved Osiris. Moderns call it a myth, yet we believed it to be true in my day. Remember that Egypt was a torrid country and her Magi were well versed in all measures tending to promote the public health. With us circumcision was a pure sanitary measure, and cleanliness the object aimed at, although the operation was practiced under guise of a religious ceremonial, so that it had both a theological and medical significance. Know, mortal, that I myself underwent the operation, and an examination of the oldest mummies found will reveal the fact that the phallic mark is common. The engraved and printed stones of any ancient country teach that this operation dates back to the most remote ages, and some vandals have lately taken from Thebes a stone representing the circumcision of the two sons of Rameses II.

"In those days, the operation was performed in the eighth year and not on the eighth day. Remember that

Moses, whose immediate ancestors were the slaves of my people at an epoch when the arts and sciences made Egypt the intellectual center of the world, was educated by the Magi of Pharaoh's court, initiated as a priest of the Sun-god Osiris, and under the name of Osarsiph acquired a full knowledge of oriental secrets. Now, this Moses had achieved great reputation for necromancy in my land; he had married, but not among his own people, and his children remained uncircumcised for many years. When Moses went to the court of the Egyptian king, in order to intercede for the freedom of the Jewish people, he worked even greater wonders than the native Magi, for when Pharaoh demanded a miracle from Moses he bid his brother Aaron cast down his rod, and lo! it was trans-formed into a living serpent, but the wise men of Egypt cast down their rods and performed the same magic ; then came another enchantment for stretching forth his hand. Aaron brought numbers of frogs from the rivers and ponds of Egypt, and the Magi repeated the same sorcery. Then followed other wonderful displays of enchantment that the wise Magi could not equal. So Pharaoh per-mitted the Jewish people to depart from the land of bond-age ; but, even after emigrating, the Jews murmured against Moses, and in order to discipline his own country-men this grand old law-giver and leader raised up myri-ads of serpents, and many Israelites died from poisonous bites. Thus was Israel delivered by Moses who had drunk the full cup of Egyptian knowledge with the three wise men of the Sublime Court of Patah, the fountain source of all occult wisdom. The exodus of the Jews oc-curred 1310 years before the Christian Era, and the line of Egyptian monarchs date back 2050 years further. Know that Moses included a vast amount of the most antiquated knowledge of my land in his teaching; for, taking advantage of his high position, he incorporated in the Pentateuch the most valuable precepts of the Nile Magi. His was a mighty mind versed in priestcraft, medicine, and statecraft, and all the mysteries of the Orient. He held one of the seven keys to the Hermetic lock, and therefore to him the true secrets of the East were as an open book. It is claimed that when Moses died his body was buried in the land of Moab, and it is written in the Hebrew chronicle, 'No man knoweth his sepulcher until this day.' Mortal, I will reveal to you a secret which has been hidden for ages: Know that what was once the mortal tenement of the Jewish leader now lies embalmed in Egypt with the Past Grand Initiates of the Sublime Court of Patah. His spirit sheds a glittering light as a divine jewel on the bosom of the Creator. He is the star of Israel. Oh! modern sage of the Order of Memphis, Mystical Recluse of Thebes! If you would solve the true riddle of the Sphinx, read the Book of the Dead."

"I have read the Bible with untiring interest," murmured Paulus Androcydes, reverently leaning his spiritual head to the Orient, "yet never dreamed of tracing back the sanitary code of Moses to an Egyptian origin, although I have agreed with many moderns that the Jewish law-giver did not originate the first five sacred books, for he always speaks of himself in the third person and seems a mere collator of ancient doctrines, usages, and statutes. He could not have even written the entire book, since a full account of his own death appears in the last chapter. I have read Herodotus regarding circumcision; but as this author wrote nine hundred years after Moses, his statement should be taken with a few grains

7

of allowance. I am aware that circumcision has been practiced for ages by the Mexican Indians, the Fijians in Polynesia, and among various tribes in Australia and Africa!"

"In my day this operation was only performed by the medical priest, for with us the priest, physician, and law-giver were one," said Athothis. "They were the potent triad created by Patah; for they were wisdom, and all wisdom is from Patah, and through all the circling ages, with few exceptions, wisdom has ruled mankind. The present day is one of these exceptions."

"Why except the present day?" asked Paulus Andro-cydes, whose curiosity was aroused. "Are not modern nations governed by wisdom?"

"No!" answered Athothis, sternly. "Scepticism now rules the world. The intelligent foresight that created what is scoffed at as superstition is no longer respected. Mankind has strayed from the paths worked out by the first inspired teachers. When mortals deny a first great cause and lose faith in a future state of happiness, wis-dom flees and morality decays. Kings' heads no longer fit the crown, and the grandest empires perish. Your modern imagines himself a God able almost to create and control natural forces. This he calls science. An initiate of the first degree, he assumes to know all the secrets of natural order. The science of modern religions that tend to materialism; the science of modern schools of medicine that are mere reflections on death; the science of modern laws that benefit the few rich and oppress the many poor—these are all vile poisonous plants, that will bear bitter fruit for future generations. The education of ears that are deaf to the inspired voices of antiquity; the education of eyes that think to discover unrevealed mysteries; the education of minds that can not reason between right and wrong—this is the false system that is undermining the very superstructure of modern society. True religion reviled; true medicine rejected; true justice ridiculed. Egypt once reached the very point for which modern civilization now struggles and fell, and the sound of that fall, though it echoed down the centuries, makes no impression on the peoples of to-day. The lesson taught mankind ages since will be repeated, and the day of social anarchy and chaos is not far distant. Osiris is setting in the west in a blood-red sky. Set, the spirit of darkness, casts the twilight of blackness over the East. Time will roll around, burying millions of mortal spirits in the deepest shadows of night. Then will the avenging Horus arise, shedding the light of a new day from the Orient; and among those who will receive a final reward are the Jews, for they have been among those who maintained a pure faith and guarded the secrets of the Egyptian temples."

Paulus Androcydes laughed scornfully, and exclaimed: "Let me hear no more of such vague mysterious prophecies. Why extol these Jews with their arrogant pretensions, their assumed martyrdom and continual poising for public sympathy, their clannish predjudices, their stupid superstitions? What have the Israelites ever done for medicine?"

"Can any intelligent man ask such a question?" quoth Athothis, in tones of surprise and disgust. "Who handed down the wisdom of other days on which all modern experience is based?"

"We had Pythagoris, Hippocrates, Herodotus, Plato, Aristotle, and a host of eminent authorities who were not Jews," answered Paulus Androcydes, proudly.

"True," replied Athothis. "Yet most of these men had an Egyptian education and the inspiration of the Orient. But who preserved even their works during the dark ages?"

"The Arabian school!" cried Paulus Androcydes, angrily. "These Israelites have never done any thing for the healing art. Name a single distinguished author they have produced."

"I might mention Moses," remarked Athothis, quietly, "or the name of the founder of the religion you profess, whose doctrine was the equality of souls before Patah— love for your fellow-man and charity. Listen to me, my mortal friend: During bye-gone ages, when Europe was steeped in the darkness of religious fanaticism and the cross went down before the crescent and turban of Mahomet; when the Christians of Spain and Portugal were the slaves of the Moors and Turks, the Jews and Arabs were the only peoples really skilled in the healing art. When the cross once more triumphed over the crescent, the Jews inherited from the Arabs what both had originally derived from Egypt; for know that the Israelites were ever intimate with the Orient—trading, speaking many languages, and ever wise. It was the Jews who preserved the manuscripts and ancient writings of the Magi and philosophers of old, and this mass of erudition included not only the learning of Egypt, Phoenicia, Assyria, and the Arabian school, but likewise the wisdom of Greece and the entire Roman Empire. They were the dealers in rare drugs and medicines, amulets, charms and magical philters. It could not be otherwise, since the Jew, above all other races, inherits the fervent imagination of Egypt. Long held in bondage among a highly cultivated people, an intellectual race that had given the world astronomy, astrology, mathematics, arithmetic, music, painting, drawing, sculpture, and architecture, in addition to systems of theology, medicine, and law, the Jews unconsciously absorbed a love for knowledge. Besides, like all other races kept in captivity, the Israelites combined ideality with natural acuteness in observation, inherent dissimulation, craft and cunning, all advantageous qualifications in days when oppression ruled; so that they became the money-lenders and really learned doctors of the world, and an ordinary saying a hundred years ago was, 'To be a Jew is to be reputed a good physician.' The skill of the child of Abraham in both these branches of business is still proverbial. 'T is true that very few Jewish doctors have left distinguished names; but name me even a few Christian moderns whose works are liable to survive the wreck of time? You have mentioned Pythagoris, Hippocrates, Herodotus, and Plato. Name me a living author of to-day whose fame will be as lasting? Know that the original teachers and discoverers of truths are never forgotten, but their disciples and imitators are lost in the mists of obscurity, shedding some faint glimpses of reflected light as they pass, but finally disappearing forever."

"Yet these Jews never had any particular skill!" exclaimed Paulus Androcydes, impatiently. "Are you ignorant of the fact that laws were frequently passed in continental Europe prohibiting Jewish doctors from practicing in Christian families, and that they were punished and driven out of many countries?"

Athothis laughed loudly, and replied: "Such enactments were indeed passed; but the Jew, as he has always done, no matter how heavy the penalty, continued to

follow his favorite profession; and popes, kings, and
emperors, in case of serious trouble, were constantly
seeking his pecuniary assistance and medical advice. I
remember an amusing instance of the latter kind. During
one of my transmigrations, I was a pet greyhound in the
palace of Francis de Vallois, King of France. My master was quite ill on one occasion, and, as his Christian
Court physicians could not cure him, although they used
enormous quantities of rare drugs, he concluded to try
a Jew. Unfortunately his Christian subjects, with the
kindly charity which they sometimes display, had driven
all the learned Israelites out of the country. So the
king was obliged to send to Spain to his royal cousin,
Charles V.; but as Charles had only one Jew left in his
realms who was really learned in medicine, he concluded
not to loan such valuable property, but sent in his place
a devout Spanish Catholic of venerable aspect and strong
Jewish features.

"When this learned Spaniard appeared before the Court,
Francis remarked: 'So you are one of those few doctors
we Christians have left who await the coming of the Messiah, as promised by Holy Writ?' To which the stupid
Andalusian replied: 'I am one of those who do not wait
for the Messiah promised by the Jewish law.' At which
the king was well pleased, thinking the man an apostate,
and exclaimed: 'You are very wise in arriving at that
conclusion.' But the Spaniard unfortunately continued:
'We Christians all know that the signs spoken of in holy
writ are accomplished!' At these words, King Francis
de Vallois flew into a terrible passion, and angrily demanded: 'You are then a Christian?' and the trembling
doctor answered: 'Yes.' Whereupon the king, sternly
pointing to his bed-room door, cried: 'Go!' Tell your

master that his failure to send me a Jewish doctor means war between France and Spain. Tell the knave that I have multitudes of Christian leeches in my kingdom and to spare, but I desired a Jew, for to my mind a Jew has more learning, acuteness, and common sense than a Christian. Go!'

"Then King Francis sent to Constantinople and obtained the loan of an extremely wise Israelite physician, who threw the Christian drugs out of the palace window, told the king he ate and drank too much, and finally ——"

"Cured him?" interrupted Paulus Androcydes, spitefully.

"Yes!" responded Athothis. "The Jew cured his Royal patient with asses milk."

"Enough!" cried Paulus Androcydes, in a bad spiritual humor. "The king must have gone back to the breast that first nourished him. Yet, changing the subject and returning to our original discourse, I am willing to admit that circumcision has latterly conferred a boon on humanity."

"How is that?" inquired the innocent Athothis.

"We use the remnants of the operation for skin grafting," answered Paulus Androcydes. Whereat, Athothis passed out of the widow, with a smile on his Egyptian face.

CHAPTER IX.

IN WHICH DOCTOR PAULUS ANDROCYDES BOASTFULLY
NAMES NUMEROUS MODERN PHYSICIANS WHO HAVE
FIGURED IN THE REALMS OF LITERATURE, AND ATHO-
THIS ADMITS THAT THE PROFESSION HAS CONTRIBUTED
SOME LITTLE TO THE STORE OF HUMAN KNOWLEDGE.

CIRCLING over the city for a few moments, the
two spirits presently alighted on a lofty church
steeple and rested on a large gilt hand, the index
finger of which pointed heavenwards. Hundreds of feet below them were busy streets, thronged
with myriads of bustling citizens and moving animals
attached to rumbling street cars and vehicles. The ringing of bells, the buzzing of machinery, and the continuous
hum of human voices commingling made a sound like
the angry roaring of a swarming bee-hive.

Perched at this altitude, Paulus Androcydes broke the
momentary silence of the upper atmosphere by indignantly remarking: "'T is strange, my Egyptian friend,
that you so constantly deride and belittle the labors of
recent workers in the field of human knowledge, attribut-
ing all valuable discoveries and classical writings to the
ancients. Speaking of the more modern medical writers
alone, without enumerating the innumerable names of
other authors who have contributed energy and vast
stores of wisdom to the scanty supply derived from
former ages, I can fairly startle you by the mere mention
of a list of famous men whose names will be heralded

with ringing notes of praise down the vast avenues of time."

" Proceed ! " exclaimed Athothis, in a tone indicating the patient exercise of enforced forbearance on the part of an intensely bored listener. " Perhaps you may be able to convince me that recent generations of doctors have been a blessing to mankind, although, I am free to confess, that I am very blind as regards this point, notwithstanding my many transmigrations."

" The doctor in medicine," said Paulus Androcydes, proudly, " has ever been the grand motor power in diffusing knowledge and enlightenment throughout Christendom ; for, owing to the strata of scepticism permeating his organization, he has caused the great changes that have occurred from time to time in the domains of law and theology. As regards these two last named professions, it has ever been the wont of their most learned teachers to accuse the doctor in medicine of iconoclastic tendencies.

"At an early date the physician acquired a taste for politics. Unwilling, however, to leave his profession for the exclusive pursuit of political existence, he was content to take only such subordinate positions as did not interfere with the duties of an active medical life.

" In the confidential capacity of physician he not only prescribed medicine but political advice, and as the recipient of state secrets from unsuspecting patients has often been enabled to checkmate the movements of popes, emperors, kings, princes, and statesmen. Under the garb of a physician, he is the true social agitator, and, to a certain extent, shapes the policy of civilized peoples, his position as disciple of the healing art protecting him

6

from the direct enmity of church and state. Quietly ag-
gressive, but with thrice the cunning and skill of the
Jesuit, he has made radical changes in the workings and
operations of ecclesiastical and civil law, and has ever
been found on the side of social revolution.

"Although crafty and usually dissimulating, he has,
nevertheless, occasionally openly entered the controver-
sial field in antagonism to the other professions. The
eminent anatomist, Michael Servetus, the author of
Trinitatis Erroribus, Dialogorum de Trinitaté, Justatitia
Regni Christi, Christianismi Restitutio, awakened the
wrath of that eminent Protestant reformer, Calvin, who
caused his medical adversary to be burned at the stake.
Remember the glorious Balthazar Orobio, who wrote Cer-
tamen Philosophicum and was so cruelly tortured by the
Spanish Inquisition, and Julian Mettrie, who was driven
out of Germany and France for merely inditing L'Homme
Machine. Look how nobly Virchow of late stood up in
the German Parliament and openly battled against the
arch fiend, Bismarck, for the cause of human right. Can
we forget Darwin, who started modern theologians with
his missing link ?

" In the field of collateral sciences, who looms up so
grandly as the doctor? Who has made botany and
natural history what they are? The study of materia
medica and comparative anatomy induces a taste for
original investigation of the flora and fauna, and many a
medical mind has been seduced from the exclusive study
of physic by that lovely syren Nature. On sea and land,
in every clime, the scientific doctor is busy searching for
new species and rare varieties. In this earnest pursuit,
he wanders from the ice-bound coasts of the Arctic regions
to the interior of tropical Africa. He leaves behind him

the tender ties of home and kindred, and too often, alas! dies of disease and want a stranger in savage lands. He it is who enriches the materia medica and supplies an unappreciative world with remedies against human ills. Among the physicians who have won unfading laurels in the botanical field only a few need be noted.

"In the early part of the sixteenth century, Leonard Fuchsias, after whom the beautiful fuchsia is called, wrote his History of Plants. In the same century Melchior Guillandius published his essay on Papyrus; Leonard Ranwolf, his Flora Orientalis; Caesaralpinus, his Treatise de Plantis; James Dalechamps, a History of Plants; John Banhinus, his Historia Plantarum Universalis; Gasper Banhinus, Theatrum Botanicum; and John Gerard, a History of Plants.

"In the seventeenth century, Maurice Hoffman wrote his Catalogus Plantarum Hortens; Prospero Alpini, De Plantis Ægypti; Ovid Montalbani, his Index Plantarium and Bibliotheca Botanica; Anthony Jusseu, his Progress of Botany; Olan Rudbeck, Catalogue of Iceland Plants; Gaspard Pelletier, Plants of Iceland; Simoni Pauli, his Flora Danica; and Leonard Plunkendt, his Almagestum Botanicum.

"In the eighteenth century, Andrew Rivinus wrote Introductio in Rem Herbarium; Michel Valentin, his Amphitheatrum Zootomicum; John Gmelin, the Siberian Flora; John Dillenius, the father of cryptogamic botany, his Catalogue of the Plants of Giessen; John Hedwig, his Cryptogamia; Nicholas Jacquin, his Floræ Austriacæ; George Oeder, Floræ Danicæ; John Zannichelli, his Catalogum Plantarum Terrestrium Marina; John Tozzetti, Usu Plantarum in Medicina; Domini Civillo, his Neapolitana Flora; Charles Allioni, his Piedmontese

Flora; George Rumphius, his Herbal Amboyana; John Burman, a Catalogue of Ceylonian Plants. In Sweden, the greatest of all botanists, the immortal Charles Linnaeus, published his numerous works. Francis Marquet wrote his Plants of Lorraine; James Spielman, the Prodromus Floræ Argentinensis; Sebastian Valliant, his Botanical Parisieuse; John Martyn, his Historia Plantarium Rariorum; William Houston, a Catalogue of Plants; John Sibthorpe, Floræ Oxoniensis; Richard Pultenay, his Progress of Botany in England; Patrick Blair, Botanic Essays; Charles Alston, his Tyrocinium Botanicum Edibergense; John Clayton, his Floræ Virginicæ; John Mitchell, the Principles of Botany.

" In the early part of the present century, James Smith published his English Botany; Dominic Villars, his Natural History of the Plants of Dauphany; Charles Wildenow, his Species Plantarum. Later, Francis Porcher wrote his Resources of Southern Fields and Forests."

"Hold!" cried Athothis. "I'll admit that modern physicians have contributed somewhat to a knowledge of botany."

"Look at the department of natural history," continued Paulus Androcydes. " In the sixteenth century, William Rondellet wrote his Ichthyology; Hippolitus Salviana, a Treatise on Fishes; Ulysses Aldrovandus, his History of Birds and Insects.

" In the seventeenth century, John Swammerdam published his General History of Insects.

" In the eighteenth century, Philbert Commerson wrote on Ichthyology; Peter Ardeti, his Bibliotheca Ichthyologica; John Fabricus, his Systema Entomologiæ; John Erxleben, his Principles of Natural History; Peter Camper, a Natural History; Hans Sloane, The Natural History of Jamaica; Edward Tyson, his Phocænia; James Smith on Lepidopterous Insects; John Berkenhout, Natural History of Great Britain and Ireland; Francis Salerme, his Animal Kingdom; John Brouguieres, on Molluscæ and Zoophylae; Louis Daubenton, in connection with Buffon, the great work on Natural History; Anthony Vallsmeri, on The Origin of Insects; Lazaras Spallanzi, and many others, on Comparative Anatomy.

"In the early part of the present century, Francis Peron published his Observations on Anthropology; Guillaume Ollivier, on Entomology; John Gilibert, on Natural History; George Shaw, Zoology of New Holland; Edward Jenner, of vaccination fame, his Natural History of the Cuckoo; James Wilkens, a Memoir on the Utility of Insects; Samuel Mitchell, his Fishes of New York; Benjamin Burton, on Rattlesnakes; and John Godman, his well known work on American Natural History.

"Within the last twenty-five years, physicians have almost monopolized the field of botany and natural history; and of late, in America alone, three superb works have been published; namely, Theodore Jasper's Birds of North America; E. Coues, North American Birds; and D. S. Jordans, Vertebrates of the Northern United States.

"In mineralogy and geology, medicine is able to boast of a Baumer, Dana, and DeWitt. In astronomy, of a Bainbridge, Toaldo, and Holyoke. In chemistry, hours could be passed in naming such men as Malouin, Bergman, Block, Darcet, Garnet, Stahl, Pemberton, Wollaston, Henry, Brugnatelli, Chaptal, Berthollet, Tennant, and Davy.

"As medical travelers and explorers, what names are

more famous than those of Varsenius, Ives, Bougainville, Petit, Park, Carver, Kane, and Livingstone ?

"In the domain of literature the doctor figures largely. The philosophic instinct of medical men is shown in the writings of Fludd, Fernel, Veethuysen, Goddard, Zwinger, Becker, Lining, Wood, Jurin, Coralli, Beccaria, Abercrombie, Galvani, Mesmer, McLean, and Bertholen.

"As a charming miscellaneous writer, the doctor stands unrivaled. In the seventeenth century, Gabriel Naude published his Life of Louis XI. and Bibliographia Politica; Guy Patin wrote his Letters; William Petty, on Political Economy; Thomas Browne, his Religio Medici; and Edward Dickinson, his Delphi Phoenicizantes.

"In the eighteenth century, Julian Freind's History of Physic, James Parsons' Affinity and Origin of the Human Languages.

"The doctor in medicine is charming as a historical writer, as witness John Caius' History of Cambridge; John Pontamus' Danish History; Robert Brady's History of England; Alexander Russell's History of Allepo; Edmund Berlace's History of Ireland; Bernard Connor's History of Poland; James Spons' History of Geneva; Oliver Goldsmith's Histories of England, Greece, and Rome; Tobias Smollet's History of England; Mathias Bell's History of Hungary; Englebert Koempher's History of Japan; Hugh Williamson's History of North Carolina; David Ramsey's History of South Carolina and the United States, Charles Bottas' History of Italy, and John W. Draper's History American Civil War.

"As a writer on antiquities, we notice the doctors' contributions in Humphrey Lhwyd's Armentaria Romano and De Mona Druidum Insular, Antiquitatæ suae Restitutæ; William Musgrave's Geta Brittanica, and William Stukeley's Itinerarium Curiosum.

"The doctor of medicine is at home when wooing the muses.

"In the seventeenth century, Antonides Vandergoes, a Dutch poet, wrote the celebrated River Y; in France, Peter Petit wrote his Codrus; Claudius Quillet, his Callapædia; Paulmier, poems in Italian, French, and Spanish; Charles Spon, the Prognostics of Hippocrates, in hexameter verse. In England, Ralph Balthurst, his Latin Poems; Samuel Garth, his Dispensary and Claremont.

"In the eighteenth century, the poetical doctor acquired undying fame. In France, Quesnoy published his well-known popular poem on The Farm House, and Herrissant an Ode to Printing. In Germany, Albert Haller wrote his Poem on the Alps; and John Zimmerman his Solitude. In Holland, John Pechlan published a laudatory Ode to Tea; and Godfrey Bidloo a volume of Low Dutch Ballads. In Italy, Marchelli indited his Miscellaneous Poems. In England, Oliver Goldsmith wrote his Deserted Village; Richard Blackmore, his Prince Arthur and Creation; John Armstrong, Economy of Love and Art of Preserving Health; John Nott, Alonzo and Leonora; Mark Akenside, Pleasures of the Imagination; Peter Templeton, his Miscellaneous Poems; Bernard Mandeville, his Fables of the Bees; George Crabbe, his Library and Village; Erasmus Darwin, his Botanic Garden. In Scotland, Thomas Brown wrote his Agnes and Paradise of Coquettes; James Granger, his Ode to Solitude. In America, John Osborn wrote his Whaling Song; Lemuel Hopkins, his Cancer Quack, and Benjamin Church numerous scattered poems.

"In the present century, in England, John Keats, a med-

ical student, published Endymion, Lamia, and Isabella;
Walcott (Peter Pindar) wrote his Lousiad; John Good,
his Lucretius; John Leydon, Scenes of Infancy; John
Aiken, Poetical Criticisms; David Moir, his Domestic Lyr-
ics. In America, Joseph Rodman Drake wrote his
American Flag and Culprit Fay, and Oliver Wendell
Holmes many delightful poems, including The Old Consti-
tution.

" Doctors Mitchell, Bigelow, Holland, Francis, and
Meigs have also been charming versifiers.

" Not content with the field of poetry, the doctor has
boldly entered the realms of fiction. We notice in the
eighteenth century, Tobias Smollet's Roderick Random,
Peregrine Pickle, Count Fathom, and Humphrey Clinker;
and Oliver Goldsmith's famous Vicar of Wakefield.

" In the present century, we had Helenus Scott's Ad-
venture of a Rupee: Warren's Diary of a Physician, and
Ten Thousand a Year; Charles Lever's Harry Lorrequer;
Charles O'Malley's Jack Hinton and Roland Cashell;
Oliver Wendell Holmes' Guardian Angel; J. G. Hol-
land's Nicholas Minturn; Weir Mitchell's In War Times,
Hammond's ' Lal,' and many others. Not satisfied with
pure fiction, the doctor has also entered the dramatic field.
Thus we see Thomas Lodge's Wounds of Civil War and
Looking Glass of London; James Drake's Sham Lawyer;
Oliver Goldsmith's She Stoops to Conquer; Benjamin
Hoadley's Suspicious Husband; George Sewall's Walter
Raleigh; Paul Hiffernan's Earl of Warwick; and Fred-
erick Pilon's He Would be a Soldier."

" Stop!" cried Athothis. " Time flies, and I weary of
your glib references. Yet, methinks you have not named
a single medical portrait painter nor sculptor whose fame
will be handed down to posterity. With all their pro-

fessed knowledge of anatomy, boastful claims to artistic eyes, and manual dexterity, the doctor in art, as in medicine, has utterly failed to treat the form divine skillfully with paint and marble—those two great agents that have so largely tended to the happiness of mankind.   Yet most modern physicians are savage art critics, and I have heard them claim that Turner had astygmatism; that Canovas Venus had a dislocated femur; that Powers' Greek Slave had a deformed pelvis, etc."

"What has the doctor done for music? What famous composers do you number in your ranks? What?"

"Hold!" exclaimed Paulus Androcydes, "your questions vex me; you are unreasonable."

Athothis laughed merrily, and said: " Strangest thing of all, you have forgotten to mention the most glorious and immortal of medical literary men."

"Who can he be?" queried Paulus Androcydes, eagerly.

"Rabelais!" answered Athothis. "He is the very prince of later writers, for he combines wit with knowledge, and to quote his words in the present instance, I may say, 'I will not launch my little skiff any further into the ocean of this wide dispute;' for when you first commenced to discourse so learnedly on the achievements of moderns, to use a Pantagruelism, 'my right entrail seemed to be widened and enlarged, which was but just now hard bound, contracted, and costive.'   I met Rabelais once during my transmigrations.   He was inhabiting the body of a dove, and was listening to Semiramis, who was inhabiting a goose at Strasbourg.   The Queen was endeavoring to convince Rabelais that Herodotus and Strabo had defamed her character, and even while in the midst of her argument was seized by the poultry dealer

8

and converted into *pate de foie gras;* for she had a true Promethean liver. As for Rabelais, he was served up the same day in a pigeon pot-pie. But come! Let us float through the windows of yonder massive building, which methinks is a hospital." So saying, the two spirits circled down from their high aerie.

CHAPTER X.

PAULUS ANDROCYDES EXTOLS THE MODERN METHOD OF
MEDICAL TEACHING, WHILE ATHOTHIS INSISTS THAT THE
SO-CALLED CHARITABLE INSTITUTION KNOWN AS A HOS-
PITAL IS RUN IN THE INTEREST OF THE DOCTOR, AND
NOT FOR THE BENEFIT OF THE SICK.

THE two spirits rested for a moment on the edge
of a mansard roof, and critically observed the
building they were about to enter. This struct-
ure was a massive collection of eight houses
separated from each other by open and arched corridors
of ornamental brick work.

"Behold the most glorious charity of our age! the
modern refuge for the poor and afflicted!" said Paulus
Androcydes, proudly. "Your ancient Egyptians never
offered such untold benefits to the sick as are presented by
our grand hospitals. Here, the many sufferers of humanity find a shelter remote from the tumult and cares of civil
life. Quietly reposing in airy rooms, on soft downy beds,
they receive the ministrations of the most learned and
skillful doctors of the state, who render their service free
of charge and from a true spirit of benevolence. Pray,
what do you think of this institution?"

"'T is a handsome piece of architecture," answered
Athothis. "Yet, methinks that those who chose the site
of the building lacked common sense. Why erect such
a charity in the heart of the dusty, noisy, overcrowded
city, where the air is murky and impure, where miasm and

fogs abound, and where even the sunlight is obscure and uncheering? Hospitals should always be located in the highlands of the country. There the air is pure, the sunshine bright, and the eyes of the sufferer may be cheered by the many verdured charms of nature, and the ear be delighted by the music of warbling birds."

"Carping again!" exclaimed Paulus Androcydes, indignantly, "'Tis a hard matter to please you, my Egyptian friend, but know there are many good reasons for locating a hospital in the city; for instance, it is more convenient for the doctors and students who attend lectures at the institution."

"Is this a hospital devoted to clinical instruction?" asked Athothis; and, even as he spoke, a loud bellowing voice echoed and re-echoed through the resounding corridors, and Paulus Androcydes whispered in an awed tone, "Hark! I hear the eloquent notes of the erudite Professor Borborygmus. Come! Let us hearken to the wisdom evolved by this sage." And the spirits entered a large hall.

On seats arranged in circles, tier above tier, were several hundred medical students, eagerly listening to the remarks of an orator, who discoursed from the amphitheater below. This individual was declaiming and widely gesticulating over a couch on which lay a pale young woman, whose deep sunken eyes, pinched features, and emaciated frame indicated the presence of some wasting malady. "I tell you, no!" shouted the lecturer. "When you are called to a case of this kind, never give ergot before making a careful examination. Sit up, Madam!" Here, Professor Borborygmus, with the assistance of a nurse and house physician, raised the trembling woman in bed, and proceeded to thump her chest and back in the most approved scientific fashion; after which, taking an exceedingly small wooden stethoscope, and applying it to the patient's heart, he listened attentively. In the meantime, the gaping crowd of students watched the sick woman with morbid curiosity. Presently, Professor Borborygmus stood erect and facing the audience, placed the index finger of his right hand on the side of his nose, gave a knowing look, and exclaimed, "Aha! 'T is as I expected. Doctor Podophyllin of the Eclectic College has made a fatal error in diagnosis. This woman has no heart disease, but caseous pneumonia, and the autopsy which will be made in a few days will reveal the truth of my assertion. I shall request Professor Postobit, our talented pathologist, to preserve the morbid specimen for the future inspection of the class." Then, turning to the nurse, he added in sepulchral tones, "Bring in the woman with cancer from Ward B!"

"Look at this intelligent class of students!" said Paulus Androcydes. "What a debt of gratitude they owe to Bottoni, De Heune, and Sylvius, the real originators of the modern clinic. Great is the public hospital, for here are exhibited, for the instruction of students, all the protean forms of disease. Here the seeker after knowledge learns from actual observation the true value of symptomatology, and the proper application of remedial agents."

"This new method of instruction is no better than the old!" observed Athothis. "The Arabian physicians and the school of Alexandria taught students in the same manner, and patients in former ages no more relished the attention of medical classes than the poor sick woman just removed from the amphitheater. This is the quietude and seclusion for the invalid of which you spoke but a few moments since. Yet, I suppose, this rolling of a patient's couch through long halls, and up and down elevators, and the excitement and fear thus engendered in the sick, is part of the treatment. This is your boasted humanity, and recalls a caustic epigram of old;

> "I'm ill, I send for Symmachus: he's here,
> A hundred students following in the rear.
> All feel my pulse, with hands as cold as snow;
> I had no fever then, *I have it now.*"

"This is a base slander!" cried Paulus Androcydes, angrily. "Has not the father of our art, Hippocrates, whom you profess to admire, claimed that clinical observation was the corner-stone in the Temple of Medical Wisdom? How can one acquire an understanding of disease without using his senses—the eye, the ear, the touch, the taste?"

"True!" retorted Athothis. "But men must learn to reason before they can observe correctly, and, as Hippocrates says, 'Even experience is deceptive and judgment difficult!' And permit me to remark that the poor woman just before the class has neither heart disease nor caseous pneumonia, but a malady peculiar to her sex, which is perfectly amenable to treatment if the wise Professor Borborygmus did but understand his trade. Yet, like most of your modern experts, this clinician has arrived at his opinion by what he considers intuition. He made no thorough examination, and, although using his sense of hearing, was unable to reason between cause and effect, and so fell into error. Of what use are these lectures, that only serve to mislead and perpetuate ignorance? What benefits do students derive when the learned professor, stethoscope in hand, informs his hearers that he detects a cardiac murmur and the patient has valvular disease? Then, too, the wise lecturer listens to ralls of many kinds, grand, gloomy, and peculiar noises, and tells the class this or that lung is diseased, but the student neither sees the malady nor hears the sounds. No hospital pathologist ever yet lived who could not relate curious tales in regard to celebrated clinician's, stories of mistaken diagnoses and most ludicrous errors. For your hospital lecturer puts his own valuation on the signification of a few symptoms, and is as apt to be wrong as right. As a man can not use his own reason, but must see things through the professor's spectacles, it follows that little good accrues either to patient or student from such instruction, and methinks that this system of medical education is justly open to criticism."

"Nonsense!" exclaimed Paulus Androcydes, in a tone of contempt and pity. "There is no better field for the exercise of reason and observation than a clinical hospital; for, even granting that men err in judgment in many cases, there are numerous instances in which their conclusions are right. The mortuary often proves that our diagnoses have been correct."

"There it is again!" said Athothis. "The mortuary! Of what benefit is a dead-house to your patients? You profess to cure. You establish hospitals for the good of the pauper sick, and not for the benefit of their medical attendants. You oblige the poor patients entering these institutions to go before classes of students, and exhibit at the sweet will of hospital managers, whose sole object is to run a so-called charity in the interest of some college. The victim of disease, dispirited and downcast, **homeless and friendless**, seeks a refuge where she **may**

die in peace; or, if beckoned on by hope, whose oft de-
lusive smile seems to urge an effort for the recovery of
health, she yields her body up to the care of the hospital
doctor, placing not only implicit confidence in his skill,
but likewise in his humanity. What kind of treatment
do these paupers receive?

Men and women of delicate frame, who need absolute
quiet and rest, are forced to submit to the trying ordeal
of a clinic. Dragged from bed to lecture-room, and from
lecture-room to ward, the injurious effects of an ever-
changing temperature, bodily disturbance, and mental excitement, are not considered as important; for the modern
view is that the patient was created for the hospital, the
hospital for the college, and the college for the professors, who pocket the students' fees. So nervous men
and hysterical women are exposed to the curious gaze of
gaping students. The private histories of unfortunate
lives are tortured out of the broken-spirited sick, and revealed to the assembled multitude. Modesty is cast to
the winds, and the poor woman patient can never look
the world in the face again without blushing. Shame on
your modern medical humanity!"

"Such remarks are outrageous," remarked Paulus Androcydes. "What right have you to judge these professors so severely? Do you desire to break up our medical schools? Do you dare to assert that there are no
humane hospital doctors?"

Athothis indulged in a spiritual sneer, and answered:
"I know full well the professional value of such men as
Borborygmus, whose principal gifts are a stentorian
voice, a voluble tongue, and arrogant vanity. With
these qualifications, and his position on the hospital staff,
he makes an impression on the unsophisticated public

and the students who sing his praises through the rural districts; for he alone hath learning, skill, large experience, and charity. You ask if I desire to break up your colleges? I answer: I have no such laudable ambition, and my time on earth is too limited to undertake such a herculean task. Medical educational institutions are to be desired, but not in connection with private corporations, that use public charities to cover their own defects. I extol those humane doctors who make daily visits to the wards of hospitals that are unconnected with clinical teaching; such men work for the love of humanity, not for self-glory or personal advertisement."

"This is most damnable doctrine to preach!" said Paulus Androcydes savagely; "and I am happy you are not a mortal; for, if you were, you would be flayed alive for such vile heresy. Know that it is easier to tear down than to build up. But, see, they are bringing in another patient."

"Let us go!" responded Athothis. "We can learn nothing from Professor Borborygmus. Come!" And as this last word echoed spiritually, the Egyptian and Paulus Androcydes floated out into the air through the mouth of a gigantic smoke-stack, and were wafted by a passing breeze to the country, among green fields and babbling brooks.

9

CHAPTER XI.

IN WHICH THE SPIRITS TAKE A RIDE BEHIND AN OLD
FASHIONED PHAETON AND OVERHEAR A CONVERSATION
BETWEEN A RURAL PRECEPTOR AND HIS STUDENT.

BELOW, lay a winding road traversing a quietly picturesque country, with long stretches of meadow land alternating with elevated knolls, on which were handsome farm-houses and capacious barns. Cattle and sheep were browsing over innumerable pastures, and the whole landscape betokened the presence of a rich agricultural and stock raising community.

"What fertile land!" said Athothis, admiringly. "It reminds me of the Nile homes in the palmy days of the first dynasty, when Egypt was truly a land of milk and honey, and these black men working in the fields are perhaps the descendants of those of our African slaves who labored under King Pepi in the eleventh dynasty."

"'Tis indeed a rich farming country!" exclaimed Paulus Androcydes, proudly. "This is the Southland, where they still live the easy patriarchal lives of their forefathers, amid lowing herds and bleating flocks; where the warm sunshine always smiles and the kindly earth yields up a never failing crop."

"Yet, even in this mundane Paradise, they have sickness, observed Athothis; "for, I notice on the highway immediately under us, an antique looking doctor's vehicle. Let us descend, and, like mischievous boys have done from the earliest dynasties, steal a ride! I see that the phaeton has two occupants."

"Can spirits ride?" asked Paulus Androcydes, in a tone of surprise.

"Spirits can ride, walk, fly, eat, drink, sleep, love and be loved," answered Athothis.

"What! eat and drink?" cried Paulus Androcydes, in amazement. "Can it be possible that immaterial bodies need material alimentation? What becomes of the unassimilated product of digestion?"

Athothis laughed merrily at this query, but responded: "Spirits have no need of food, but can gratify their tastes and desires, even as mortals, if it please them so to do. I might assert, for instance, that the April showers that bring forth May flowers are merely the result of spiritual renal action, but forbear, lest I be accused of indelicacy. Here is the phaeton! Let us ride on the old fashioned spiral rear springs." And, even as he spoke, the spirits took their places on the end of the slowly moving vehicle.

The mortal occupants of the phaeton were two plainly dressed men: one gray bearded, with really handsome features, healthy ruddy complexion and clear blue eyes; the other, a young man of two and twenty, with dark complexion and luminous bright orbs. They were evidently discussing the medical profession; for as the spirits arrived, the older man was remarking: "I believe the vast majority of practitioners are satisfied with merely telling patients their ailments."

"That may be true, Doctor Rusticus," answered the younger individual; "yet no patient is satisfied unless his physicians make a diagnosis, for when a man is ill and sends for a medical adviser he invariably inquires, 'Doctor, what ails me?' as though the physician's opinion would make one of the laity any the wiser. Thus, the medical attendant may say, ' You have liver complaint,' and the invalid is satisfied ; for, knowing that every man has a liver, and that in the natural course of events the hepatic organ, like other viscera, is liable to disease, the sufferer's curiosity is gratified, and his mind placed at ease."

" Precisely so !" replied Doctor Rusticus ; " and, therefore, I argue 't is bad policy to gratify a patient's morbid curiosity, unless the subject of disease be a person of intelligence and phlegmatic temperament, for the human imagination in the vast number of persons is exceedingly vivid, and your client is apt to magnify the importance of his symptoms. Thus, out of a really insignificant affection, serious organic troubles may be induced. I have known patients whom doctors had declared weak lunged, die of hasty consumption, when really at its onset the complaint was a trifling bronchitis. I have observed men die of heart disease and apoplexy, in order to ratify the previously expressed opinions of some practitioner in whom they had confidence. The effect of mind on matter have never been sufficiently studied. I contend that a true doctor should quiet the anxiety of his patient before remedial agents can be successfully employed."

" I fear," said the student doubtingly, " that you agree with Broussais that the real science of medicine consists in the art of cheering the sick with—with hope."

" You are partially right," responded Doctor Rusticus ; " and I insist that it is the duty of the physician to cure his patient, and not merely express what the laity consider a scientific opinion ; for what, after all, do one's patients know of medical theories ? I find in my practice that those who have implicit confidence in my professional skill, who take their medicine in faith, asking no

questions, are usually the ones to recover. It is your
sceptical and morbidly curious who suffer and become the
prey of veritable maladies. Remember, when you start
out in practice, that you are the doctor, and no matter
what your client's social or political position, do not, under any circumstances, humor his whims; for if you do,
he will at once imagine that he knows as much about his
ailment and its treatment as his medical attendant, and
you will have in him a stubborn and ignorant consult-
ant."

"Listen!" cried Athothis, approvingly. "Here is a
good teacher of the healing art. One year in a buggy
with such a wise old preceptor is worth three years in a
modern medical college."

"How absurd," retorted Paulus Androcydes, "for
such a preceptor is a poor instructor when he claims that
imagination can produce heart disease, consumption, and
the rest of the maladies that prey on mortals. But,
hark ! Doctor Rusticus is braying again."

"When you go to the medical college of Utopia," continued Doctor Rusticus, "do not be led away by the
erratic brilliancy of young lecturers who, at the present
day, become professors after practicing for two years,
whose learning and experience in the healing art is not
as great as the unsophisticated public mind imagines.
These young savants who quote lists of foreign authors
a yard long in order to sustain the wildest assertions;
these medical parrots who, poised on college perches, discuss with intense volubility of the progress made by
medical science. Do not permit such downy chinned
sages to sap the present sound judgment you possess,
nor be not molded to their views, since the theories they
enunciate are ever as transitory and changing as those of

the authors they follow. Sift the few grains of wheat
from the mass of chaff; recollecting, meanwhile, that the
wisest and hardest working doctors that ever lived only
acquired small knowledge after years spent in contemplation. Frequent your dissecting-room, and study well
your anatomy and physiology, perusing the works of
standard writers only—those writings that time and experience have shown to be the best. Forget not that the
medicine of to-day is overcrowded with incorrect physiological and pathological reflections that tend to the ex-
clusion of a dignified system of therapeutics; for recent
works on materia medica and therapeutics are the mere
dogmatic utterances of a few experimentalists, whose
conclusions are based largely on erroneous observation—
methods that really deal with abstruse chemico-patho-
logical questions viewed from an experimental stand-
point. I believe that eight out of ten people dying at
the present day perish not as much from ignorance in
diagnosis as from a want of proper therapeutic knowledge
and common sense on the part of so-called scientific
practitioners."

"Your opinion is to be respected," quoth the student;
"but, nevertheless, you seem to favor the views of Boer-
haave, who insists that all the good a few true Æscula-
pians have done for mankind has been more than offset
by a multitude of pretenders whose reasoning being
fallacious redounds to the injury rather than the benefit
of humanity; yet a study of vital statistics fully evidences the fact that the average longevity of our modern
people has been increased since medicine became a
science, and not a mere empirical art. What stronger
proof can any intelligent mind demand? For, in all
candor, you must confess that the practitioner of to-day

is better drilled and schooled in the requirements of his profession than the physician of fifty years ago. At present, the public requires a highly cultured man as medical attendant, and not the dull and sleepy fellow who formerly played nurse to his patients, and boasted that all medical wisdom was founded on experience."

"How absurd!" exclaimed Doctor Rusticus. "What ancient statistics have you to prove your wild assertion that the average longevity of man has been increased? Yet, even granting your proposition, for the sake of argument, do you mean to contend that the institutions and asylums maintained for the care of the maimed, the blind, the deaf, the dumb, and the insane, have not been important factors in securing such a result? Besides, in ancient times, there were vast losses of human lives from wars and wide-spread famines. No! Religion and human charity have done more to increase longevity, if such increase can be proven, than all your boasted discoveries in medicine. Cholera, small-pox, and yellow fever are just as malignant now as they ever were, and only need a start to show how impotent is physic to prevent their sway. You allude to the better education and higher mental qualifications of your modern doctor. This is the pretentious claim of the faculty of to-day. Now, I am seventy years of age, and, when a young man, started out in life with a fair classical education, acquired by candle-light, and not under the domes of Starved University or Fail College. I read Greek and Latin at sight, and, on graduating at Philadelphia, wrote my thesis in one of the now truly dead languages. At the present day such ancient tongues are mysteries to your average practitioner. An amusing instance of this fact fell under my notice some two years since when Squire Cloverblossom, whom we are now on our way to visit, insisted on my sending to Utopia for two eminent physicians to meet me in consultation over his wife. These two M.D.'s, who likewise signed A.M.'s after their names, came at my summons, lured on by the prospect of a large fee, and we consulted. They shook their heads wisely, leaving the impression on the Cloverblossom family that I was ignorant of the nature of the malady, pronounced the case to be one of angina pectoris, when it was really pericarditis; prescribed a strong solution of nitro-glycerine; charged a hundred dollars each for their science, more than I ever mulcted the Cloverblossoms for in a whole year's constant service; and then started with me to catch a home-bound train. On the road to the station, they discoursed gravely and learnedly on the physiological action of glonoin, and finally got into a controversy on the subject of homeopathy, in which Hahnemann was soundly abused as the first authority on the doctrine of similars. 'Gentlemen!' said I, interrupting the discussion, that had become violent. 'Gentlemen!' said I, unable to restrain my amazement, not only at their ignorance, but total want of logic. 'Gentlemen!' said I, 'are you not aware that Hippocrates first used the aphorism "*vomitus vomitu curatur,*" which is simply equivalent to "*similia similibus curantur,*" and is therefore neither recent or new.' Whereat the two young professors tried to look very solemn, and one of them remarked, 'Please express yourself in German, as that is the classical medical language. We do not understand *Greek.*' And yet these two men attached the degree of A.M. to their names."

The student laughed gently at the anecdote, as did

Paulus Androcydes, but it was noticeable that Doctor Rusticus and Athothis maintained a dignified silence.

"Did Mrs. Cloverblossom recover?" asked the student, assuming his wonted air of gravity.

"No!" replied Doctor Rusticus, crustily. "She went off! How could it be otherwise, since the city doctors loaded the poor woman with nitro-glycerine? However, her husband must have been satisfied with the treatment, as he has since married a girl some forty years his junior."

"How abundant the dandelions are this spring!" cried the student, with the evident intention of changing the subject.

"Yes!" answered Doctor Rusticus, glancing at the numerous yellow flowers fringing the green grass at the road-side. "It is one of our most reliable indigenous remedial agents. What a pity that it is not more used. Its golden imbricated florets mark the coming of spring almost as surely as the incoming swallows. There is no agent I am acquainted with so useful in real chronic pulmonic affections and diseases of the liver as the fluid extract of taraxicum. How beautiful the dogwood looks with its snow white blossoms. I have known the bark of this tree to break up severe cases of ague where quinine failed. It seems as though an ever-kindly nature furnishes mankind with the very remedies needed in cases of sickness, and, strange to say, these medicines are usually most common in localities where the diseases for which they are useful are most prevalent. Malaria and liver complaint are frequent causes of indisposition in this valley, and these specifics are growing on the same soil; but here we are at Cloverblossom's gate, and now we will go in and examine our patient." Together, student and preceptor alighted, crossed a blue-grass lawn, and entered a handsome farm-house, closely followed by Athothis and Paulus Androcydes.

CHAPTER XII.

ATHOTHIS, TO IIIS SURPRISE, REDISCOVERS ONE OF THE
LOST ARTS.

IN a large front room, seated in an easy-chair, was a strong, robust looking man, aged about sixty years, with flushed face and bloodshot eyes. This individual gazed around angrily as the physician approached his chair, and remarked in a tone of evident irritation: "I thought you would never come! My headache's much worse than yesterday, and my ears still keep buzzing. I was so dizzy this morning on rising, that I fairly staggered across the room. Doctor, you must help my head immediately, or I shall go mad!"

"Yes," added a pert-looking young woman, standing at the back of the farmer's chair, bathing his forehead; "do give my husband some quieting medicine! I'm fairly tired out waiting on him. He is very cross, and keeps complaining of numbness in his leg."

"My first wife had more patience than Maria," remarked Cloverblossom, chidingly.

"It's a pity she died!" retorted the woman, spitefully. "You worried the life out of her; but I'm not one of the meek kind. I never had any patience with old men. I told you that before you married me."

"If it had not been for those city doctors, Laura would have been here to cheer and comfort me now," moaned the farmer, shaking his head despondingly, while large tears started from his eyes.

"I don't think you regret Laura's death more than I do!" cried the irate young wife, casting a bewitching glance at the student. "They say 't is better to be an old man's darling than a young. man's slave. Some old maid must have originated that idea. I wish your first wife was here to attend to you."

At this instant a captive female redbird, in a wicker cage at the window, hopped about nervously and twittered wildly.

"Observe the action of the feathered prisoner," said Athothis to Paulus Androcydes. "That poor little female bird is now inhabited by the spirit of Cloverblossom's first wife; and she is grieving at her inability to minister to her former husband's wants, and is crying in the language of the redbird tribe, 'Oh! my well beloved! Oh! could you but know that I am here!'"

Dr. Rusticus did not appear to heed the family jarring of the Cloverblossoms, but continued to make a careful examination of the patient's chest and pulse, finally silencing the woman by saying, in a calm voice, "Your husband is a very sick man, Madam! Go to the kitchen at once, and bring me an old tin basin!"

"What in the world does he desire to do with a tin basin?" demanded Paulus Androcydes of Athothis.

"Wait and see!" replied the Egyptian. "But observe that he is rolling up the farmer's shirt sleeve, and is placing a rubber bandage around his arm, above the elbow. Tell me, my mortal friend, what is your diagnosis in this case?"

"I judge that the patient is threatened with meningitis," answered Paulus Androcydes.

"You are not far from right," observed Athothis, approvingly; "inasmuch as you have located a portion of the disease in the patient's head; but cast your spiritual vision not only over the cerebral mass contained in the cranium, but likewise glance at the contents of the thoracic cavity. Notice how the vessels of the brain are enlarged and distended; but, above all, observe the disturbed action of the sick man's heart. See the left-sided hypertrophy of the latter organ—watch its rapid pulsations and how at every systole the tension on the arteries of the brain is increased. If the patient is not soon relieved some vessel in the cerebrum will be ruptured, and what will follow?"

"Apoplexy and consecutive paralysis," responded Paulus Androcydes, eagerly watching the disturbed vital action in the human organism before him.

"Ah! here is the woman with the basin," said Athothis. "Now, carefully observe the action of this wise old country practitioner."

Dr. Rusticus now handed the basin to the attentive student, and asked the farmer to grasp the side rounds of his chair firmly ; then, with a rapid motion, plunged a bright thumb lancet into the median cephalic vein of the farmer's right arm. A stream of dark red blood spurted from the opening, and fell into the uplifted basin.

"Why, this must be venesection!" exclaimed Paulus Androcydes, excitedly. "'Tis the first time in my professional career that I have had the pleasure of witnessing this operation of antiquity."

"Methought 'twas one of the lost arts," murmured Athothis. "Yet bleeding is one of the most valuable therapeutic agents ever given to mankind."

"I always agreed with Van Helmont that blood-letting is injurious," observed Paulus Androcydes, softly.

"Van Helmont was a mere imitator of Erasistratus,"

retorted Athothis. "He knew not the value of a really sovereign remedy. But listen to the remarks of Doctor Rusticus to his student, and you will learn much, for methinks this honest old country practitioner, judging from his keen medical discernment and prompt action, has saved the patient's life."

"Never hesitate to bleed freely in such cases," remarked Doctor Rusticus to his student. "When you find a full, hard, bounding pulse, blood-shot eyes and congested face, use your lancet promptly; it is the only true remedy in such an emergency. In performing this operation, I advise you to follow the directions laid down by Antyllus or Albucasis, for no authors have written more clearly on this subject. Apply your inch and a half bandage tightly when you bleed from the arm, and do not use the lancet until the veins are swollen and prominent."

"Look!" said Paulus Androcydes, in evident spiritual delight. "The flush is disappearing from the patient's face, the brain is less engorged, the heart's action not so tumultuous as a few moments since. This is indeed marvelous. Hereafter, I shall be the strong advocate of blood-letting, though modern medical scientists teach that vene-section is a dangerous remedy."

"It is dangerous in unskillful hands, as is any remedy," replied Athothis. "And, because it was too often abused and misused by ignorant men, it fell into disrepute. Yet, moderns have made a mistake in wholly discarding such a remarkable curative procedure. Did not Hippocrates commend bleeding? Has not Celsus claimed it to be a specific for numerous ailments? But, see! Doctor Rusticus is now securing the patient's arm with a bandage placed over a compress soaked in cold spring water, and Cloverblossom is much relieved, for he is saying, 'My headache is entirely gone, and I feel like a new man.'

"Ah! my mortal friend, you must study up this subject and carefully weigh the wise utterances of Hippocrates, Galen, Celsus, Aetius, Avicenna, Rhazes, and Albucasis, who were among the early writers on this now all but lost art. This patient will never recover from his heart disease, but will probably live for many years, thanks to the skill of Doctor Rusticus. What hosts of full-blooded people, who so frequently die of apoplexy, might be saved did the practitioner of the present day but know the value of venesection. Yes, the death rate from brain troubles and pneumonia has largely increased since bleeding was discarded and quinine became the fashionable remedy. Sooner or later, the latter agent, although of immense value, will be omitted in practice, because its baleful and injurious effects are commencing to be noticed. How happy this student should be with such a wise old preceptor, whose lips drop the golden words of long garnered wisdom, whose heart is free from deceit, who strives to learn from a sheer love for knowledge, who labors to cure his patients, and wastes no time in meditations on death. This is a real doctor; yet, methinks Rusticus would starve to death in a city where his ideas and methods would be considered old and obsolete. But, come! it must be late, and I would fain inhale the fragrant odors from a well-kept dining-table; for really, I am spiritually hungry."

"Do you desire dinner?" asked Paulus Androcydes, laughingly. "'Tis something remarkable to dine spiritually ; nevertheless, as I wish to learn a few things from experience, I will accompany you most cheerfully."

"Away!" answered Athothis. And soon the two spirits once more hovered over a smoky city, and descending, passed down a flue into a fine restaurant.

CHAPTER XIII.

IN WHICH ATHOTHIS AND PAULUS ANDROCYDES DISCUSS A MODERN DINNER AND THE SUBJECT OF DIET.

N entering, Athothis and Paulus Androcydes seated themselves at a well laden table as two jolly *bon vivants* were about to commence an epicurean onslaught on several well prepared and savory dishes, the delicious perfume and spicy odors of which would have tickled the spiritual palate of Heliogabalus. "I feel the fragrant aroma of this dinner permeating and filling my gastronomic soul with delight," said Paulus Androcydes joyfully. "Oh, this is bliss! How delightful this immaterial appetite! Only to think, in my mortal habitation, I suffered from dyspepsia, and many years since was forced to forswear good dinners; but now I am absorbing the very essence and active principles of stewed terrapin, and am truly happy. Oh! this reminds me of old times! Do you enjoy the same amount of ecstatic pleasure, my Egyptian friend?"

" 'T is, indeed, a much more satisfactory way of dining than that of the material state," answered Athothis; "for in our present condition we neither have to swallow nor chew, and there are no rumbling nor grumbling intestines to disturb. Yes, spiritual digestion is truly æsthetic and refined. One has the keen sense of taste increased a hundred-fold, without the vulgar necessity of really physically eating and drinking."

10

"This is probably the enjoyable condition alluded to in '*De Rerum Natura*,'" observed Paulus Androcydes, "where it says:

"'Odors incessantly stream from many things,
  As doth the cold from the river,
  As doth the heat from the sun,
  As doth the spray from the sea,
  That crumbler of walls on the shore,
  As the moist flavor of salt,
  As we wander beside the green waves—'"

"Stop!" cried Athothis. "Methinks the classical Lucretius would not relish such a rendition of his lines."

"Nevertheless, this well expresses my peculiar sensation of taste at this moment," responded Paulus Androcydes; "for it is so closely allied with the olfactory sense that I can not distinguish the difference. Ah! this spiritual gustatory faculty is entrancing! Oh! this is divine rapture! I inhale the delicious fragrance of this stew, and believe more than ever that there is no soup-making aliment equal to turtle flesh."

"Egypt was the land of terrapin," said Athothis, sadly; "yet with us it was not considered a luxury, and I never did fancy the dish. Besides the two turtles, from which this stew was made, were inhabited but yesterday by Epicurus and Chrysippus. They were captured by a bare-legged fisher-boy, while quarreling as to the use of human flesh as an article of diet, Chrysippus insisting that such meat, when properly prepared, was most excellent."

"Having finished the soup, let us devote our attention to oysters," remarked Paulus Androcydes, smacking his spiritual lips. "These bivalves are the delicate creatures which Matron eulogizes as 'sea truffles,' although I must confess that I observe not the resemblance in flavor of oysters and fungi. Avicenna claims that truffles cause paralysis; oysters on the half-shell do no such mischief. Rhazes insisted that oysters should be cooked in oil and seasoned with assafœtidæ, and knew not the dainty things were most easily digested when raw. Juvenal says of Montanus:

> " 'And in my time, none understood so well
> The science of good eating. He could tell
> At the first relish, if his oysters fed
> On the Rutupian or the Lucerne bed.' "

" What a clever thing of old Baron Cuvier to steal his classification from Aristotle—the ὀστρακόδερμα. But notice these two gentlemen with whom we are dining; they are following the advice, laid down by Galen, and eating young radishes before commencing solid food. Ah! what a magnificent fish!"

" I detest fish!" exclaimed Athothis, as a cover was removed, revealing a splendid specimen of the finny tribe. "So far I have not relished this repast. Such fish were not eaten in my day, as they were supposed to contain the evil spirit of Typhon."

" Yet, like the modern Jew, you seem to enjoy oysters," observed Paulus Androcydes, tauntingly. " I would fain declaim against your Egyptian prejudices as Anaxandrides, saying: " You worship an ox; I sacrifice him to the Gods. You consider an eel a demon; we think it by far the best of fish. You do not eat swine's flesh; I am passionately fond of so doing."

" But what was esteemed by Grecians was despised by other races," retorted Athothis; " for your fastidious Romans, like the Egyptians and Jews, held eels in contempt, while all ancient races detested the frog, which appears to be represented at this dining board. Indeed, the blood of the red frog was a deadly poison under the first dynasty. The Greeks, Romans, and even many Jews, were fond of scale fish; and these animals, pickled, are used every Friday night on the tables of modern Hebrews. Such learned writers as Xenocrates and Athenæus were deeply versed in the art of pickling fish. The ancients considered boiling the best way to prepare this food for delicate stomachs, and claim that even an ostrich is unable to digest the fried variety. There is but little nourishment in fish. The Ichthyophagi, described by Herodotus and Diodorus, while apparently healthy, were short-lived; and the opinion, expressed by some latter-day psychologists and physiologists, that fish is brain food, will not hold good, as exclusively fish-eating peoples are not only weak-minded, but leprous, becoming scaly, like the animals they devour. No race, following an exclusive diet, ever exhibits genius. The Galactophagi, among whom may be enumerated the Abii, were mostly celibates and enemies of war, very effeminate and cowardly. Beef-eating races are usually savage and brave—like Achilles, who was fed by Chiron on the marrow of wild beasts."

"Milk is a fine food, however," said Paulus Andro-cydes. "In spite of the statements of Hippocrates, Galen, and Celsus, that it produces headache, billious-ness, and flatulence, I have constantly given it in my practice as a remedy for Bright's disease—knowing full well that the ancients decried its use by those suffering from complaints of the kidneys and bladder. I usually give it boiled in cases of consumption, and find when it is heated with hot iron, in the form of a red poker, as recommended by Serapion, that it contains enough of

the metal to make a good tonic. But the fish before us
is not an eel, my friend, but a pike—such a one as
Archestratus was wont to call 'a gift from the gods.'
Inhale its invigorating fragrance, and do not imagine,
because it is highly seasoned, that the salt thereon is
following your ancient belief—the saliva of Set."

"Sneer not at my people on account of their prejudices!" answered Athothis. "Though I will admit that
the Egyptians, as well as the Jews, disliked the admixture
of salt with certain varieties of food. We were superstitious, like all learned races ever are, but our prejudices
were really the outcome of real wisdom, for only highly
intellectual people have enough imagination to believe in
things supernatural."

"Yet, I am very sceptical, as regards the utility of
certain Egyptian prejudices," remarked Paulus Androcydes, "and do not wonder that the Jews, whose
instructors you claim to be, have so many stupid customs.
I am enjoying the pike, and you await the next course,
which, as I live! is a choice Westphalia ham. See! one
of the gentlemen is carving a slice of pink pig meat."

"Westphalia ham!" exclaimed Athothis, in spiritual
disgust. "Of all vile food on earth, this is the worst.
Are you aware, unhappy mortal, of the perils that linger
in this meat?"

"It is so delicious, that I shall discard the fish, and
take in the exquisite aroma of swine flesh!" retorted
Paulus Androcydes. "I would brave many dangers for
a dish like this! But why are the celebrated smoked
joints of Westphalia more injurious than other meat of
the same variety?"

"In Westphalia," responded Athothis, disdainfully,
"they nourish and fatten their hogs on human offal, and

this fact is so notorious that Chamouzet proposed to have droves of swine follow armies, and for sanitary purposes, as well as utility, to use this flesh, fed on excrement. As for my Egyptian prejudices against pork, it dates back to the first dynasty. Know, mortal, that the evil spirit Set, after tearing the eye out of Horus, was changed into a pig, and my people, therefore, had no love for an animal inhabited by a demon. The Jews inherited this dislike of pork from the Egyptians, and Moses, in the eleventh chapter of Leviticus, states that 'the swine, though he divide the hoof and be cloven footed, yet he cheweth not the cud; he is unclean to you. Of their flesh ye shall not eat, and their carcasses shall ye not touch. They are unclean to you.'"

"What an absurdity!" laughed Paulus Androcydes, scornfully. "What intelligent modern would dare to affirm that the spirit of a demon could be driven into a hog?"

"Christians of to-day," answered Athothis, "believe in the eighth chapter of Saint Matthew, and therein it is told how Christ, traveling through the Gergesene's country, met two men, possessed of devils, who begged to be relieved, and 'there was a good way off from them a herd of many swine, feeding. So the devils besought him, saying, if thou cast us out, suffer us to go into the herd of swine.' Christ granted the devils' request, thus fully evidencing his true Jewish dislike for pork."

"I have earned this reply," said Paulus Androcydes, apologetically, "and, as a good Christian, can no longer doubt that swine flesh is unhealthy. Yet ancient medical writers extolled its use: Hippocrates claimed it was wholesome; Galen that it was nutritious, and 'tasted like human flesh;' while Celsus loudly praises the delicate food. The Arabian school of doctors did not commend pork so highly, for Rhazes ignores the mere mention of such meat; but that was on account of the religious prejudices he held in common with the Egyptians and Jews."

"Yes," added Athothis; "even your moderns now acknowledge the hog genesis of the *Echinococcus cysticercus* and *tœnia solium*, while latterly the subject of *trichina* has awakened attention. These low forms of animal life abound in pork and constitute real demons of disease. They are destroyed by the high temperature used in cooking. This is the only reason that prevents the wide spread of terrible maladies. Doctor Gordon has shown that in Upper India the English soldiers, who frequently eat *measley* pork, that contains an abundance of *cysticerci*, suffer greatly from tape-worms—it being calculated that thirty-three per cent of the troops are thus affected. Whereas, the native Hindoos and Mohammedans, who rarely, if ever, touch swine flesh, have a comparative immunity from such affections. The negroes and poor whites of the Western and Southern American States, who are exceedingly fond of pig meat, and buy spoiled pork from unscrupulous dealers, die of tape-worm by the hundreds. This is the boasted civilization of the nineteenth century. And with all these alleged scientific discoveries you have not the ordinary common sense of ancient savages; for, knowing full well the dangers of such a diet, you glut your sensual appetite, and take the risks of incurring leprosy, scrofula, trichinosis, hydatids, and tape-worms. Believe me, that many of your cases of so-called typhoid fever, meningitis, abscess of the liver, and insanity, may be traced to a pork diet."

" But many Jews die from these diseases !" interrupted
Paulus Androcydes.

" True " replied Athothis. " But not at all in proportion to population. Besides, these affections are
sometimes propagated in other ways. This is only one
of many superstitions, founded on wisdom, to enable
man to live longer."

" The waiter has taken the Westphalia ham !"
remarked Paulus Androcydes, with a spiritual sigh of
relief. " Behold ! the covers are removed from a pair of
dainty quails and a tender spring chicken. We are also
to have venison and egg sauce !"

" I prefer quail. They are old-time Egyptian
friends !" said Athothis. " Yet, methinks these two
gentlemen, with whom we are dining, reverse the ancient
custom, which was to serve the quail in fruit jellies as a
dessert at the end of a meal."

" I prefer my quail stewed, and not broiled," quoth
Paulus Androcydes. "And, following the directions
laid down by Apicius, that famous gourmand in the court
of Augustus, I believe that this delightful game should
be cooked in a gravy, composed of salt, pepper, borage,
fine mint, and a little honey, stirred up with oil and rich
fruity wine, in equal proportions. As for spring chick-
ens, they are fit only for invalids, and an admirable food
for him that hath a delicate stomach. The venison looks
tempting, but I fully agree with Rhazes, who insists
that such meat is difficult to digest, although Celsus holds
a contrary opinion. The egg sauce looks tempting, yet
such food may really possess some of the medicinal
qualities ascribed by the immortal Pliny. I suppose
that your ancient Egyptians had an aversion to flesh, as
well as fish ? Am I right ?"

"Many species of birds and animals were served in my time," answered Athothis; "for instance, the hawk, heron, lapwing, swallow, crane, etc. Yet we Nile dwellers were passionately fond of eggs; and the first artificial incubators were the sun-heated hatching-ovens of Egypt. We learned this wisdom from the ostrich, which deposits its eggs in the warm sand. As articles of diet we avoided, like modern Hindoos and Jews, the flesh of all carnivorous and insectivorous birds. You have probably noted the similarity in the hygienic precepts, formulated in the book of Leviticus and the Code of Menu. Moses declared that the eagle, osprey, vulture, kite, raven, owl, nighthawk, swan, pelican, stork, heron, lapwing, bat, etc., were entirely unfit for human food; and you must admit that even the Christian masses share in this belief and prejudice at the present day. As for animals, my people avoided eating the *canidæ* and *felidæ*. With us the dog was typical of Sirius, the barker, whose appearance in the heavens was an unfailing omen that the annual overflow of the Nile had commenced. The cat was sacred to the moon, and during the first dynasty, as now, repeated its midnight prayers to the lunar deities. The weasel was also affected by moonlight, and its liver was said to contract and expand at certain lunar periods. As for rats, they were a pest in Egypt, and were hated by every good Nile dweller, for they were enemies of the Sun-god Ra. The prejudices derived by Moses from the Egyptians are the same as those noted among the Hindoos, for the ' rules of Menu ' assert : 'Let any twice born man avoid carnivorous birds, and such as live in towns, and animals with uncloven hoofs, except those allowed by the Vedas. The sparrow and the plover, the Brah-

11

many goose, the vulture, the crane, the woodpecker and
parrot, male and female, birds that strike with their
beaks, webfooted birds, the lapwing, those that wound
with strong talons, those that dive for fish, the heron, the
raven, all amphibious fish eaters, tame hogs and fish,
and—' "

"Cease !" cried Paulus Androcydes. "Do you desire
to rob mankind of all the flesh foods? Do you expect
moderns to take up all these ancient prejudices? Is the
world to become as abstemious as Iccus, that fool doctor,
who ate little or nothing, in order to live, and died like
the rest of humanity? Methinks that Egyptian superstitions, like spirits, have transmigrated from age to age
in various disguises, and it is high time for modern
science to call a halt."

"Let modern people violate our ancient rules and
sanitary regulations and suffer the consequences,"
responded Athothis, defiantly. "They dare not! lest a
multitude of new plagues are sent to pester them."

"Yet wise men have scoffed at such regulations,"
replied Paulus Androcydes. "Hippocrates believed in
using pigeons, partridges, ducks, and geese, and his views
were coincided in by Galen, Ætius, and Rhazes,
although these writers admitted that water fowls are not
as cleanly as land birds. The praises of woodcock have
been sung by such delightful poets as Horace and Mar-
tial, while the thrush is spoken of by Perseus, who says:

> " 'To use my fortune, Bassus, I intend :
> Nor therefore deem me too profuse, my friend,
> So prodigally vain, as to afford
> The costly turbot for my freedmen's board;
> Or so expert in flavors as to show
> How by the relish *thrush* from *thrush*, I know.'

"The Romans ate blackbirds, Galen enjoyed broiled sparrows and well roasted bustards, Athenæus doted on roast swan and broiled crane, while a favorite dish with gourmand emperors was stewed heron tongue. I know that Seb, the father of Osiris, is usually depicted with a goose egg on his head, and that in Burmah it is claimed that this bird laid the cosmic egg, and 'tis true this cackling, waddling animal once saved Rome; yet we still continue to serve the eggs up in omelets, and swallow its diseased liver with avidity. I know that Brahma rode on the goose Hansa; that the fish, Matsya; the turtle, Kurma; the hog, Varaha, are among the ten incarnations of Vishnu. I am also aware that Siva is typified by a bull, Vishnu by an eagle, Indra by an elephant, Ganesa by a rat, Varuna by a fish."

"Enough !" exclaimed Athothis; "for here before us are delicious spring vegetables—tender asparagi and delicate spinach, fresh lettuce with water cresses, boiled turnips and stewed parsnips."

"The odor is divine !" said Paulus Androcydes. "But I love the lettuce above all for its quiet and soporific qualities. Galen cured himself of insomnia with the delicious lactucarium; and, rubbed on the head, Florentinus claimed that it allayed his headaches and produced pleasant sleep. These asparagi are indeed juicy and the very food that Simeon Seth contends have all the nourishing qualities of meat."

"Beware !" cried Athothis. "Remember that asparagi are violently diuretic, and that the spinach, though boiled, is, according to Haly Abbas, a quick laxative."

"But these asparagi are dressed with caper sauce, which is all in good keeping and taste, since capers, according to Serapion, strengthen the stomach, and are likewise recommended by Galen for obstruction of the liver and spleen."

"Hold!" exclaimed Athothis. "I fear you have studied your stomach more than any other part of the anatomy. Yet, as Bacchus in 'The Frogs' of Aristophanes cried to Hercules, so I cry to thee, 'Teach me to dine!' But one thing is lacking at the festal board : where is the wine?"

Paulus Androcydes laughed good-humoredly, and answered : "You forget, my Egyptian friend, that we are not among a wine drinking people. In this country our ideas of public morality are such that we do not drink openly. We keep our private bottles, or we take our stimulants in quiet bar-rooms or isolated beer-halls, and at dinner-tables strive to appear sober. The pale-faced man, by whom you are seated, is the Reverend Timotheus St. John, rector of All Innocent's Church. This poor clergyman would not dare to taste wine publicly, lest he might be scandalized and accused of open dissipation ; even when he takes a little brandy with his quinine, following the popular prescription (for, like many clergymen, he suffers from malaria) ; he bars his study door, pulls down the blinds, and gropes on the dusty upper shelf of his library, where, concealed behind five cumbrous volumes on 'Infant Baptism,' he finds the mysterious flask that contains a potent remedy, and swallows it without water. The bald-headed, red-faced man, sitting at my side, is the Honorable R. R. Subsidy, formerly a senator, but now a candidate for any thing that pays. He is an astute lawyer and fine politician, intelligent enough to know the difference between a retainer and contingent fee. He can not drink in public at present, as he is up before the people for an office, and the opposition newspapers might publish some sensational story in regard to his having been seen under the influence of liquor. He really needs the ministration of the clergy, and so has asked the Reverend Timotheus Saint John to break bread with him."

"Here come beautiful red strawberries, green Malaga grapes, and golden oranges!" exclaimed Athothis.

"The fruit is delicious," replied Paulus Androcydes. "The grapes are from sunny Spain, and, if we are to believe Galen, should be eaten at the beginning of a meal, and not at the *mensa secunda*. These strawberries would have inspired Virgil and Ovid to sing their praises anew. Strange fact, that no very ancient writers mention the orange."

"What is this white, sugar-sprinkled mass of half-baked flour?" inquired Athothis, trembling in spiritual fear, as a chop-whiskered waiter in swallow-tail coat deposited the pastry on the table.

"That," answered Paulus Androcydes," in a tone of triumph, "that mass of unripe apples and tenacious dough is the greatest of modern inventions in the interest of the doctor. That is the glorious pie of my native land."

"What a pie!" cried Athothis. "Can it be that I see that most horrible invention of Set for destroying the human stomach? Quick, my friend, let us fly from this dreadful place! For know, that if pork hath killed its hundreds, pie hath slain its thousands. Away! away!" And the two spirits flew out of the restaurant so rapidly as to create a whirlwind, blowing over a wooden sign

at the front door, inscribed, "Hot meals at all hours."
Whereat, the proprietor of the house remarked to the
cashier, "It's regular March weather this April," and
replaced the advertisement.

CHAPTER XIV.

PAULUS ANDROCYDES BEHOLDS THE WONDERS OF THE
MODERN MEDICAL LABORATORY, AND ATHOTHIS INSISTS
THAT THE TRIBE OF MORTAL FOOLS, INSTEAD OF
BECOMING EXTINCT, HAS MULTIPLIED.

SCENT the odor of medicine!" cried Athothis, as the two spirits spun through the air. " Ah! here is a place of safety." And these words had scarcely fallen from his spiritual lips, than they passed into a magnificent stone-front building.

"What have we here?" demanded Paulus Androcydes, glancing about in intense curiosity.

"I should judge we are in a modern medical laboratory," replied Athothis. "And observing the enormous tanks and retorts, filled with strange mixtures, I am led to believe that the owner of this mammoth establishment hath an immense number of patients. There are enough tinctures, extracts, elixirs, syrups, and pills to slay an army. This is the wholesale medical compounding business."

"Great heavens!" exclaimed Paulus Androcydes, in alarm. "Have we escaped the dangers of green-apple pie in order to undergo the perils of patent medicine? Quick! my Egyptian friend! Let us fly from this den of knavish quacks; for should my professional confreres learn that I have merely visited here, I should probably be expelled from the Philautian Medical Society, of which I am, at present, an honorable member."

"Nay! Let us tarry a moment," expostulated Athothis. "Why would your merely looking into the mysteries of this trade lead to your expulsion from your profession?"

"I should be violating that most sacred of earthly things, our Code of Ethics," responded Paulus Androcydes, solemnly, "and would deserve the most severe censure. Know, that our great contract is, not to associate with charlatans."

"And do you live up to the requirements of this wonderful agreement?" asked Athothis, in a voice of compassion.

"I strive to live up to the rules," answered Paulus Androcydes, with dignity.

"Nevertheless, you meet the worst pretenders and most ignorant practitioners daily in professional intercourse," retorted Athothis, sternly. "The older members of your societies are eternally preaching what they do not practice, i. e., medical honesty. Your code, as now construed by the mass of doctors, means hypocrisy in business—the senior taking advantage of the junior on every possible occasion. Quiet your spiritual conscience; for, I assure you, our being here is a mere accident, and we may learn something even in such a shop. For instance, note the accurate system and order maintained; observe the various and ingenious mechanical appliances for bottling, labeling, and wrapping the murderous nostrums. This branch of popular medicine is well worth a philosophic study. Here physic is reduced to a science. This is the school of specifics. Look at the hundreds of loaded down shelves, and read the ornamental labels, printed in the highest style of art, in order to attract the curious eyes of the ever credulous and ignorant masses. See how all the packages are arranged alphabetically, and even the alliterative titles thereon are seducing. Behold!

> " Æsculapian Asthmatic Antidote,
> Boerhaave's Bilious Bitters,
> Celsus' Consumptive Cure,
> Dioscorides' Diarrhœa Destroyer,
> Eustachius' Empyema Eradicator,
> Fallopius' Famous Febrifuge,
> Galen's Genuine Germicide,
> Hipprocates' Hemorrhoid Healer,

"And other three-worded titles, too numerous to mention. Gaze at the four-lettered symbols, on the other side of the room :

> " Nostradamus' Natural Neurotic Nervine,
> Orbasius' Original Ovule Obstruent,
> Paracelsus' Patent Persuading Pills,
> Quesnoy's Quick Quinsy Quieter,

"And the five-worded enigmas :

> " Rhazes' Remarkable Rheumatic Resolvent Remedy,
> Sydenham's Superb Strong Scrofula Specific.

" Note the whole alphabet of six-lettered emblems, as for example :

> " Vesalius' Very Valuable Vaunted Volatile Vermifuge—"

" Stop !" cried Paulus Androcydes, in a tone of despair. " It would take a year's time to read all these strangely constructed remedial names."

" Yet these things are wonderfully interesting to an Egyptian of the first dynasty, as evidences of the growth of popular intelligence, and a proof that the human mind, though sceptical in regard to religion, hath an ever increasing faith in the marvels wrought by physic," murmured Athothis. " In my day people did not take drugs as a regular article of diet. The result was, our physicians had but little to do. I now understand why modern practitioners are so numerous and so busy. Know, mortal, that you should encourage, rather than discountenance, the manufacture of these nostrums. Make mankind believe in medicine, whether it be practiced wholesale or retail. In this room alone are poisons sufficient to undermine ten thousand healthy constitutions. Yea! every bottle sold will make patients for your glorious profession."

"I admire your gentle irony," said Paulus Androcydes, smiling spiritually. "Yet, this state of public affairs vexes me exceedingly, inasmuch as these patent medicine interests are largely fostered by our eminent divines, legal statesmen, and highly intellectual newspaper editors."

"Behold the indorsement on the bottles of Hippocrates' Hemorrhoid Healer," said Athothis. "Here are the names of farmers and merchants by the score. Listen, while I read a few of these certificates:

"AMOOSEGEAPOLIS, MAINE.
"DOCTOR CHARLATAN.

"*Sir:* After taking seven bottles (price, $1.50 each) of your valuable Hippocrates' Hemorrhoid Healer, I completely recovered from my malady, and for the first time in years preached a really eloquent sermon last Sabbath. Your remedy is a gift from Providence, and I shall advise my congregation to use the same.
"Yours truly,
"D. VINE GOSLING, D. D.
"P. S.—Send me another full case by express, C. O. D.

"BOURBONVILLE, KENTUCKY.
"DOCTOR CHARLATAN.

"*Dear Sir:* I joined the temperance society of this city, a short time since, a total wreck in mind and body, from the disease known as hemorrhoids. I was in miserable health until last week, when, noticing your advertisement in the *Christian Chronicle of the Cross*, I purchased three bottles of the marvelous remedy. I had hardly taken the first swallow of medicine, when I felt like another man. I went to court immediately, and my argument in the case was so overpowering and eloquent, that the jurymen acquitted my client without leaving the box. After the verdict, I invited the judge to my residence, and we finished the two remaining bottles. Hereafter, your valuable specific shall never be absent from my side-board.

"Respectfully,

"LEX. BARRISTER, Attorney."

"Wonderful! most wonderful!" gasped Paulus Androcydes, in tones of mock admiration. "Yet, I am satisfied, and you need not read the thousands of similar indorsements, which have made Doctor Charlatan's medicines famous. Yet, methinks the ingredients of such remedies should not be kept secret, lest their talented compounder might die, and the world be left desolate. Knowest thou the composition of these specifics, my Egyptian friend? Name! oh, name! I pray thee, what is contained in these admixtures?"

"These medicines are for the most part alcohol, to which different poisons are added," answered Athothis. "Common whisky, epsom salts, and glucose are the principal remedial agents in Hippocrates' Hemorrhoid Healer."

"Curious how so many people, who advocate temperance, enjoy their stimulants in the shape of medicine," remarked Paulus Androcydes. "Not very surprising, after all, that the columns of religious newspapers are full of fulsome notices of such panaceas. However, as you remarked, this is the age of progress, a century that boasts of its culture and intelligence. The dawn of patent theology and patent law can not be far off."

"Nonsense!" responded Athothis. "Such trivial
matters as this should not weary your mind and produce headache. Cheer up, my mortal friend!"

"Such remarks neither comfort me nor remedy the
evil," said Paulus Androcydes, shaking his spiritual head
in sadness. "For myself, I can not help but condemn
the growth of the evil, and believe with Yorick, who,
speaking of this species of medical murder, remarked :
'The life of our neighbor is shortened, and often taken
away, as directly as if by a weapon, by the empirical
sale of nostrums and patent medicines, which ignorance
and avarice blend. The loud tongue of the quack im-
prudently promises much, and the ears of the sick are
ever open. As many of these pretenders deal in edge
tools, too many, I fear, perish from their misapplication.
So great are the difficulties of tracing out the hidden
causes of the evils, to which this frame of ours is subject, that the most candid of the profession have ever
allowed and lamented how unavoidably they are in the
dark, so that the best medicines, administered with the
wisest heads, shall often do the mischief they are in-
tended to prevent. These are misfortunes to which we
are subject in this state of darkness. But when men,
without skill, without education, without knowledge,
either of the disease, or even of what they sell, make
merchandise of the miserable, and, from a dishonest
principle, trifle with the pain of the unfortunate, too
often with their lives, and from the mere motive of dishonest gain : every such instance of a person bereft of
life, by the hand of ignorance, can be considered in no
other light than a branch of the same root. It is murder
in the true sense, which, though not cognizable by the

law, by the laws of right, to every man's own mind and conscience, must appear equally black and detestable.'"

Athothis indulged in a light ripple of laughter, and replied: "The author whom you have just quoted is too sentimental, and the man of the world to-day smiles in contempt at such silly moralizing. 'T is true that only clergymen may preach, and only lawyers are permitted to plead, while every man and woman in the land has a right to practice physic; but so long as the tribe of human fools is increased, so much the better for your profession, which, in the end, reaps all the reward. What you consider an evil is the doctors' blessing in disguise, inasmuch as a spread of medical ignorance increases human woe. In my mortal days we had, as I stated before, no patent medicines; but now, thanks to modern chemistry, linked with the commercial spirit, the food you eat and the wines you drink are adulterated and drugged. Your people are fond of being deceived, and the sharpness of your nation in matters of trade is proverbial. They are fond of proprietary medicines and impure food; and as the country is one of universal liberty, can think and choose for themselves; as all men are born, according to your constitution, 'free and equal,' no leadership is required. Your so-called statesmen are guided by the masses, in place of being trusted advisers."

"Say naught against my Government!" cried Paulus Androcydes, angrily. "Yet I am free to admit that our high public officers should regulate the sale of poisons and adulterated food, and should severely punish men who injure the health of their fellow-citizens."

"Which would be wholly inconsistent," retorted Athothis, "since the Government itself issues debased coin, and therefore officially sanctions adulteration. But who is that well-dressed, pensive-looking individual, leaning over his desk in evident mental trouble ?"

"That is Charlatan, the owner of this establishment. He is thinking of his daughter, who is now lying dangerously ill with fever," responded Paulus Androcydes.

"Is he giving her some of his own remedies?" asked Athothis.

"No!" replied Paulus Androcydes. "Charlatan's family never use quack medicine. He employs Billem and Pillem."

"It amounts to the same thing," observed Athothis. "But, let us fly hence!"

CHAPTER XV.

ATHOTHIS SNEERS AT THE GERM THEORY, AND AROUSES
THE ANGER OF PAULUS ANDROCYDES, WHO CONTENDS
FOR THE MODERN OPINION.

"THERE goes Doctor Slasher!" exclaimed Paulus Androcydes, as the two spirits floated across a broad avenue. "See his magnificent equipage as it stops in front of the Hotel Nicholas. Professor Slasher is one of the most prominent of modern surgeons, and lectures in the medical college of Utopia. He has ligated the aorta, excised the cerebrum, removed the liver, trimmed the semi-lunar valves, and stretched the pneumogastric nerve. He was the first operator to cut out the stomach, kidneys, and bladder. His reputation is wide-spread, and has already brought him numerous patients from abroad."

"Are his operations usually successful? Does he remove the patient, as well as morbid viscera?" demanded Athothis.

"I must admit!" answered Paulus Androcydes, after a few seconds hesitation, "that the subjects of these capital surgical manipulations usually require the after-assistance of an undertaker, and are wont to seek the quiet seclusion of the churchyard. Nevertheless, his cases, at best, are hopeless."

"In other words, he has built his reputation on the dead," retorted Athothis. "And his epitaph to fame is inscribed on the tombstones of humanity. Admit, my mortal friend, that Doctor Slasher usually hastens transmigration, instead of keeping life in its original habitation? Perhaps Slasher is about to perform some other wonderfully skillful operation on suffering mankind, as I notice he has in his company two young physicians, evidently assistants. Let us follow him!" And in a few seconds the little party entered a superbly furnished *suite* of front rooms.

Lying on a velvet-covered sofa, in a chamber facing the west, was a beautiful child of seven summers, with light flaxen hair, clear blue eyes, rounded and dimpled face flushed with fever and excitement. Kneeling by the child was a sweet-faced, but care-worn, woman in tears, who, clasping the tiny hands of the terror-haunted baby, was whispering words of comfort and encouragement to the little one. " Do n't be frightened, my darling," she softly murmured, as the thoughtless physicians gravely arranged their cases of terrible instruments in full view of the patient. "Mamma will not leave you, and these good doctors have only come to make you well. Be a good little girl, and you shall have a new dolly and ever so many pretty dresses."

" These gentlemen are about to perform tracheotomy," remarked Paulus Androcydes. " This is evidently one of those cases of membraneous croup in which an early operation offers the only chance for life."

" I suppose these modern practitioners would scorn an emetic," quoth Athothis, " and prefer to cut the baby's throat, in the interest of science and self-glory, in order to report the result of the operation at the next meeting of the Philautian Medical Society."

"They are now administering chloroform," responded Paulus Androcydes; "and soon the little one will be unconscious of all pain. Ah! my Egyptian friend! the ancients never knew the marvels of anæsthesia."

"We had the *lapis memphiticus*," answered Athothis, dryly, "the which, when taken in a little wine, destroyed all physical sensibility, without blunting the mental faculties. See how this poor child struggles, cries, and gasps in terror and pain, as the surgeons hold it down, preparatory to using the poisonous vapor. The child is now insensible and livid; and what is that curious apparatus that projects a minute shower of spray over the patient's uncovered throat, as the surgeon's knife penetrates the tender young tissues?"

"That," replied Paulus Androcydes, proudly, "is another triumph of modern surgery. 'T is carbolic acid spray, thrown from an atomizer, to scare off and destroy all germs which have the audacity to linger in the vicinity of the gaping incision; for, alarmed at the presence of this potent agent, the low forms of animal life will retire to a safe distance, and all danger of infection is past."

"This reminds me of the Chinese, who beat gongs and fire off shooting-crackers, to keep away the demons of the air," murmured Athothis, quietly. "And their remedy is equally as efficacious. Cast your spiritual vision through the bodies of these surgeons, and see contained therein precisely the same low organisms as are observed in the child. Yet, they claim to be healthy, while the little one is ill. Look through the atmosphere of the room, and out in the open air beyond, and you will notice billions on billions of organizations exhaled from the animal and vegetable kingdoms. Each breath inspired

12

by man contains countless myriads of such animated forms."

"What!" exclaimed Paulus Androcydes, in surprise and violent indignation. "Do you dare to insinuate that our modern germ theory is false? Ah! my Egyptian growler, no fact is better established in our noble science than that disease is entirely dependent on the morbific action exercised by these minute organisms. Let us reason on our point logically. I boldly assert, if there be no germs in disease, all diseases are germless. Something can not be induced by nothing. Nor can that which has no existence be developed into what is, *ergo*, you must grant that to produce what has no existence is an impossibility. Now, reversing this proposition, according to the same subtile reasoning, I assert that it has been demonstrated that disease is dependent on germs. Therefore, all maladies are germ diseases ; for something will produce a similar something. That which exists is redeveloped into what is, *ergo*, all that exists had a pre-existence."

"Stop!" shouted Athothis. "If you had lived under the first dynasty, an immense pyramid would have been erected to your memory. Such logical reasoning is truly wonderful, and might induce germs of thought of new form, the bacilli of a diseased imagination."

"You are personal!" cried Paulus Androcydes, wrathfully, "and will not listen to the voice of reason."

"What reason or logic is there in the causation of disease?" retorted Athothis.

"I believe in the germ theory as I do in my own existence," answered Paulus Androcydes, growing more and more enraged. "I have seen germs with my own eyes, on a microscopic slide, and can not doubt my own senses. I know their haunts and habits, and have closely studied their numerous forms. Take the disease called erysipelas, for instance; are you not aware that in this malady micrococci are found in the lymph vessels of the skin?"

"Does that prove that the organisms cause the disease?" demanded Athothis.

"Yes!" responded Paulus Androcydes, in a decided and very positive tone. "Because, after carefully excluding the erysipelas micrococci from other bacteria, you may raise a pure breed of these animals, which, being introduced into the human body, produce erysipelas. Can you any longer doubt that this disease is due to a special germ?"

"Such reasoning renders me even more sceptical," answered Athothis; "for, methinks any organism derived from morbific matter inherits the toxic properties of its genetic source, and that the strength of its poisonous principle may be attenuated in direct ratio as the so-called germ is removed from primal influences. I remember once, when I inhabited the body of a rabbit, that I partook very freely of belladonna berries, and, while thus employed, was shot by a hunter, who, together with his family, feasted on my flesh. Two of this poor man's children died of eating me. Now, I contend that rabbit meat is not in itself unhealthy food. Yet, it sometimes engenders belladonna poisoning."

"Aha!" cried Paulus Androcydes, "you will presently commit yourself to the modern theory."

"Never!" said Athothis, firmly. "While I do not deny that many low organisms are apparent in conditions of disease, I contend that they are the result and not the cause of morbific action. According to this same pretty theory, you would be forced to admit that these germ organisms, like all other animated creatures, are likewise subject to sickness, and that their diseases are germ diseases, dependent on germs that in themselves are diseased, and so on to infinity. Thus, we might say, behold a bacillus suffering from the micrococci of erysipelas, or, lo ! an innocent bacteria dying from tubercular bacilli. Where is the human eye that can penetrate the mysteries of Patah? Bah ! your modern scientists, in their infantile efforts to grasp the hidden secrets of nature, remind me of the babe that, lying in its mother's arms, stretches its puny hands heavenward, in a vain attempt to grasp the crescent moon."

" Rank heresy !" exclaimed Paulus Androcydes, in a tone of passion. " Your comparisons are not only absurd, but unfair. Look at the magnificent achievements of modern science. Take, for example, that extremely fashionable disease for which mercury is the true specific. Therein, Donne found the charming *vibrio lineola* in the sores ; Hallier discovered *micrococci* in the blood ; Klatch noticed spores ; Lorstorfer stumbled on round granules ; Cutter observed *mycelia*."

" Hold !" retorted Athothis, " what particular organism caused this entrancing malady ?"

" Behold our glorious Pasteur and Koch," continued Paulus Androcydes, without apparently noticing the interruption. " Who discovered the cause of disease in the silk-worm, the grape wine, and sheep? What is modern science without the tubercle germ and the comma baccillus ? How could we live without them ?"

" You mean, how could we die without them ?" replied Athothis, laughingly. " I must say that I admire the business methods of French and German savants, since their generous Governments now pension such true scientists. But, tell me, my mortal friend, why Finkler and Pryer, who found a comma bacillus in diarrhœa, are not likewise rewarded."

"Their bacilli were lemon-shaped," answered Paulus Androcydes, testily.

"From which remark I infer that the form of the germ has much to do with the nature of the disease," remarked Athothis, meekly. "Yet, I would respectfully inquire, are not cholera subjects found, in which the disease germs are absent?"

"There are exceptions to all rules," said Paulus Androcydes, in a tone of disdain.

"Was not the cholera bacillus found in Egypt different from that found in India?" queried Athothis, in evident amusement.

"I am not on the witness stand?" cried Paulus Androcydes, in a fury. "'T is useless to discuss the subject of the germ theory further. Look! Doctor Slasher has inserted a tube in the child's throat, and the operation is over. Observe the marked improvement in the patient's respiration. She no longer gasps for air; but, with a sweet smile on her innocent baby face, slumbers peacefully."

"And will never wake again in her present habitation," added Athothis, bitterly; "for, observe, the little one's brain is engorged and congested. She has been overpowered by the anæsthetic. The lungs are slowly expanding and contracting, while the poor baby heart is fluttering. If Doctors Soother and Rusticus had had charge of this case, this lamb would never have been slaughtered. As it is, these scientific butchers will fill a once happy household with sorrow, and break a mother's heart; for the poor woman will not long survive the loss of her little one."

" 'T is an easy matter to abuse the profession," quoth Paulus Androcydes, sneeringly. "Ah! my wonderful, talented, gifted, and intellectual Egyptian friend, tell me truly, what was the cause of sickness in this child? Know, that these skillful surgeons have only performed a simple operation, by means of which they hoped to save life."

"And yet have driven it out of its primal abode!" answered Athothis. "You ask for the original cause of the disease, and I answer, poisonous air and water!" And as he spoke the Egyptian's spiritual finger pointed directly at a stationary washstand in the corner of the room.

" I can readily believe that such may be the case," remarked Paulus Androcydes, "since sewer gas contains poisonous germs. Yet, this hotel is provided with the best sanitary plumbing. No better evidence of modern mechanical skill can be found than in the plumbing noticeable here. It is simply perfect. The luxury and convenience of our house-drainage system can never be appreciated by one of the first dynasty."

"We had no plumbers in Egypt," responded Athothis, with dignity; "for we knew full well that filth was the prime factor in the causation of disease, and had no need for the services of mechanics who convert house interiors into sewers. 'T is possible, in this respect, that we lacked the rare wisdom displayed by the present age. Now, as filth is the chief agent in creating sickness, it follows that the more cleanly a population, the less its mortality rate. The experience of centuries has shown that man is a most uncleanly animal. So from the dawn of creation, laws have been enacted to enforce habits of personal purity. Strange fact, that the fundamental principles of sanitation derived from the Egyptians may be found formulated in the Mosaic Code; and this document and Code of Menu have never been improved, notwithstanding the boasted progress of sanitation in the last two hundred years. The practical views of the Jews, obtained from my people, are still the foundation-stones of public hygiene; and the precepts enunciated by the Bible contain the very essence of all sanitary knowledge. This hygiene of ages past has been of more real utility to man than the quack sanitary regulations of the present day, which are for the most part conceived in the interests of architects, contractors, builders, and plumbers, who proclaim that their methods are scientific. Your modern medical sanitarian encourages these impostors and destroyers of life, by claiming that all causes of morbific action are dependent on specific germs, invisible to the naked eye, but capable of being observed under the microscope; germs whose toxic properties may be increased or diminished at pleasure by means of culture; germs which may be propagated or destroyed, following the desire of the investigator, claiming that these minute organisms are the *cause* and not the *result* of disease. Their views have been accepted by the vast majority of physicians and the laity as final and conclusive, not only on account of their plausibility, but also for their adaptability to medical usage, as the germ theory serves as a cloak under which to hide professional ignorance. The world can not see the germs floating around in the atmosphere, but the doctor assures it that the little infecting demons are there as thick as the sands on old ocean's beach; and it is at this point that modern

medical science invokes the aid of the chemist, and the
two form an alliance with sanitary engineers and plumbers. Hundreds of antiseptics and disinfectants are
thrown on the market for sale to the gullible portion of
the community, the vast mass of whom are led to believe,
through newspaper advertisements and printed circulars,
that disease germs are killed and frightened away by
such agents, for instance, as carbolic acid and chloride
of zinc. Now, these drugs are valuable remedies for
abating nuisances, undoubtedly, and it is often necessary
to destroy offensive and disagreeable odors; but when
the fears and credulity of the public are worked on, in
order to sell the products of the laboratory, such medical
practice must be classed among the Black Arts, and is
really rank charlatanism. This is indeed the science of
combining medicine with profit. Your modern architect,
in company with the sanitary expert, designs healthy
homes (?), with all the luxuries and improvements of the
period, including that precious boon to suffering humanity, the water-closet system, which work is usually
placed in the hands of highly educated and refined plumbers. Thousands of devices for ventilation and sewage
are duly entered at the Patent Office, and, curious to
state, all these inventions are directed toward the exclu-
sion of supposed germs from house interiors. Even
water-pipes are arranged with a view of preventing the
ingress of the little devils of disease from the atmosphere
surrounding, while a contaminated water supply, filled
with these same germs, derived from streams foul with
polluted sewage, circulates freely within the pipes,
and is largely used for potable and bathing purposes.
Sewers are the home and paradise of these so-called dis-

ease germs. Yet, modern scientists, believing in this doctrine, invoke the aid of water-closets and stationary wash-stands, and assure the credulous public that sewer gas is harmless when perfectly filtered through water traps and germ-preventive taps."

"Stop!" cried Paulus Androcydes, in a fury. "Do you wish to destroy public confidence in our present system of house drainage and disposal of excreta? Do you desire to ruin our plumbers and sanitary experts, by such false and malicious assertions. Know, my Egyptian friend, that I have an interest in two water traps and a patent sewer-pipe."

"Aha! aha!" laughed Athothis, blinking his spiritual eyes in merriment. "I now perceive why you are such a warm advocate of the germ theory. Besides, you forget the large annual income you derive from those of your clients who are poisoned by sewer gas and polluted water. However, if modern peoples are willing to admit that sewer gas is poison, either from its germs or other inherent toxic properties, and encourage the introduction of zymotic diseases into their households, even submitting to the enactment of laws forcing property-holders to open sewers in their bed-rooms and kitchens, I do not think that an old Egyptian of the first dynasty need grieve; for, after all, these modern sanitary appliances only tend to hasten primal transmigration, as they have admirably done in the case of this little child, who is now about to quit her mortal tenement; for, look! she is passing out!"

The last rays of the setting sun kissed the face of the baby girl, who, reclining against the warm, tender bosom from which she had drawn life, gasped feebly at long in-

13

tervals, while the once bright, laughing, blue eyes were now unlighted, set, and glazing.

"Notice the cocoon hanging against the open window-sill! See! it is moving," said Athothis.

"I do!" exclaimed Paulus Androcydes, in amazement, as a vapory form seemed to issue from the child's body and, contracting almost instantly into a minute spark of light, flashed across the room and disappeared in the cocoon. At the same instant a beautiful white moth burst forth from its covering, and floated away on the golden mists of the evening, growing smaller, smaller, and smaller, until lost from sight in the fading sunset.

"Is this a first transmigration?" asked Paulus Androcydes, as a great awe fell over his spiritual being.

"It is!" replied Athothis, solemnly, "and a sight vouchsafed only to a few mortals—the initiated in the Circle of Thrice-Chosen Seers of Memphis."

"My child! my darling! Oh! my poor baby is dead!" moaned the grief-stricken mother, holding the empty earthly casket, and kissing the inanimate features.

"If she only knew!" continued the Egyptian, in a gentle tone of pity. "But soon she, too, will pass from the first degree and enter the mysteries; for, has it not been written, 'Oh! death, where is thy sting? Oh! grave, where is thy victory?'"

"Do you believe in spiritualism?" demanded Paulus Androcydes, eyeing Athothis with eager curiosity.

"Can I doubt my present state?" responded the Egyptian. "If you but knew! But seek not to know too much of the future—enjoy the present, forget the sorrows of the past."

"I can take you to a spiritual *seance* this very evening," said Paulus Androcydes, "and will show you the marvelous power possessed by a certain medium."

"Lead on!" cried Athothis, laughingly. "I would fain enjoy one of your modern performances; and perhaps mortals may have learned more of these manifestations than we knew under the first dynasty." And as these words were spoken Athothis and Paulus Androcydes once more traveled through space.

CHAPTER XVI.

ATHOTHIS AND PAULUS ANDROCYDES VISIT AN INNER
CIRCLE OF MODERN MAGI, AND VIEW THE MYSTERIES
OF SO-CALLED SPIRITUAL MANIFESTATIONS.

THE sun had now disappeared below the horizon,
and the West was robed in purple and scarlet
fringed with gold. "Behold the divine light of
Osiris fading from the world, while Set, the
Prince of Darkness, casts his baleful shadows o'er the
East," said Athothis, mournfully. "Another day has
passed and night approaches. Now, in the melancholy
twilight, the spirits of fallen angels emerge from their
hiding-places in the forests, lakes, and rivers, from the
damp, moldy grave-yards and charnel-houses of extinct
humanity, and, in forms visible and invisible to mortals,
stalk abroad, growing bolder and more defiant as the
glory of Ra is further removed. In the fathomless ocean
of space about us float innumerable aerial apparitions,
demons inhabited by damned souls doomed to destruction. Note, in the large public park beneath, how
nymphs and naiads lasciviously disport their half-scaled
bodies on the surface of the miniature lake. Listen to
the amorous sighing of fauns and satyrs in yonder ver-
dure-embowered grove, while pixies and hobgoblins scam-
per over the greensward, and wildly circle and waltz
under the dew-sprinkled flowers."

"What nonsense!" exclaimed Paulus Androcydes.
"You are striving to frighten me. I am no believer in

such absurd doctrines, and, though I see the strange sights you mention, nevertheless deem them but transitory illusions. Like the immortal Paracelsus, I labor under an hallucination, and think I view objects that have no real existence. These airy phantoms are mere creatures of the imagination, conjured up by an over-excited brain. You speak of fallen angels and spirits of the damned. As for the ghosts of men, be they good or bad, quitting their graves to haunt their friends, I believe it not; neither do I admit that our blessed dead in any manner mingle in the affairs of this world."

"Seeing, you do not believe," said Athothis. "Methought, when you invited me to a seance, that you were not sceptical in this regard. Are you aware that at this very moment you pass through space with me? Do you doubt your own spiritual identity?"

"Perhaps I am dreaming," answered Paulus Androcydes, " and mine are but the vivid mental impressions of a restless cerebrum. Yet, I honestly affirm myself to be in a sad state of bewilderment, and am filled with terror as night creeps over us, and the air grows chilly as a shroud."

"Doubting mortal!" cried Athothis, reprovingly. "Have no fears, for I promise to return you safely to your original habitation, where, on what you deem an awakening, your perplexity will be still more profound; for, like the majority of moderns, you will doubt your own senses on points clearly perceived by the ancients."

"I confess to seeing," replied Paulus Androcydes, " yet I may not be awake, but mentally dreaming." At this instant a pair of bats flew across his spiritual face, while an owl hooted loudly from the gnarled branches of an oak beneath. Paulus Androcydes drew back in affright, while a tremor permeated his being, and he cried aloud, " This is reality ! I fear bats and detest owls."

" Yet these animated natural forms are no more distinct than the other visible shapes plainly hovering around in the air," observed Athothis.

" They are equally apparent," whispered Paulus Androcydes, with timidity; "but I still doubt my vision, though I shudder with horror."

" Courage ! " said Athothis, cheeringly, at the same time uttering a low, musical laugh that sounded like the æolian murmur of an evening zephyr. " Ah ! this must be the abiding place of a medium, for look at the swarms of sprites and goblins climbing through the window cracks and key-holes."

" 'T is the home of the healing medium, Professor Diabolus," replied Paulus Androcydes ; "and he is said to work wonders with the sick."

" He hath an appropriate name," quoth Athothis ; " and 't is easy to cure diseases dependent on a vivid imagination, when the patient hath implicit confidence in the power of the medium." The two spirits now hovered over a large cut-stone residence, on the outskirts of the Park. This building, surmounted by a steep slate roof, faced to the southwest, and commanded a magnificent twilight view of the misty hills, at whose base flowed a mysterious river. "Let us enter!" continued the Egyptian ; " for now I shall witness a *seance* by your much-vaunted modern magi, who can not do their work in the full sunlight like the necromancers of my day, but are yet quite clever in their manifestations. After all, such exhibitions of trickery and supernatural power combined are best carried on under cover of Set, who is the true patron of the art. Under the first dynasty

we controlled the demons. Our magi were men of
mighty intellect and will power, who commanded the
presence of subjects from Amento through the Grand
Master Osiris. Your medium of to-day is almost always
an ignorant and sensual male, who has bartered his soul
with Typhon, in order to secure limited power and the
gratification of his appetites. Other mediums are highly
organized and nervous women, whose movements are controlled and directed by fiends from the outer darkness.
Female mediums are, however, unconscious deceivers,
inasmuch as, owing to their greater amount of credulity,
they are more easily imposed on and trifled with by the
disciples of Set ; and, believing truly that they hold con-
verse with the souls of the blessed departed, mislead not
only themselves, but many weak-minded and overcurious
people, upsetting human reason by creating doubt."

"Lead on!" exclaimed Paulus Androcydes, impatiently ; "for I fain would witness these manifestations
from a true spiritual stand-point. If this is true, I shall
learn something; if it be disordered fancy, I shall laugh
on awakening. One thought encourages me, even in my
present state of mind : that is, you do not seem to
approve of the methods of these mediumistic impostors,
and are therefore a safe guide ; and though Galen laughs
spirits to scorn, I will follow thee, oh ! mighty Egyptian
necromancer."

"The learned Pythagoris, Socrates, and Plato—all
names universally respected—taught many truths regarding these mysteries," remarked Athothis, softly, "while
those truly gifted ecclesiastical writers, Austin and Ter-
tullian, were firm believers that such demonstrations
caused mischief, and that the ghosts that appear to mankind are usually wicked apparitions. Austin, in fact,

taught that these demons strove to overthrow and destroy human happiness with false doctrines. Pythagoris and Plato possessed strong mediumistic power, and invoked the presence of these evil phantoms at will. They learned the art in Egypt, where, instructed by the Brotherhood of the Sphinx, they took the 85° as Grand Masters of the Memphian Magic."

"Enough!" cried Paulus Androcydes; "for, by the spirit of the demon who lurked at the sword-hilt of Paracelsus, I swear to unravel this mystery; and should I become infected with this strange malady known as spiritualism, I shall, on my return to physical life, resort to the remedies prescribed for such an affliction by Avicenna, Rhazes, and Sennertus. Yet, tell me before we enter the mansion of Professor Diabolus, how, on awakening, I may test the truth of these mysteries?"

" Should you wish to invoke the presence of these demons," said Athothis, " remember that they always assume the appearance of mortals when presenting themselves to human eyes. Should you desire to see the apparition of some departed friend, gaze fixedly on the bright, shining sun for the space of five minutes, in the meantime concentrating your mind on your friend as he appeared in life; then quickly darken the room, and lo! standing before you will be the counterpart of him you desire to meet."

" This is shallow trickery," responded Paulus Androcydes, " and a mere illusion caused by the combined action of an irritated retina on an overexcited mind. Besides, such a test might induce blindness, owing to the dazzling brightness of the sun's rays on weak eyes."

" To see these ghostly shadows at night," continued Athothis, endeavoring to restrain a spiritual smile, " follow the directions laid down by Albertus Magnus; use his celebrated collyrium, that consists of the right eye of a hedge-hog boiled in oil and kept for some time in—"

"Nonsense!" interrupted Paulus Androcydes. "I have no faith in such procedures. Yet, I have secretly experimented in the materialization of flowers and plants, taking the ashes of such forms of vegetation, following the formulæ laid down by D'Israeli in his 'Curiosities of Literature.' But these were merely the tricks originated by overcredulous and imaginative chemists.

"In order to discover whether modern mediums are guilty of deceitful practices, I have thought that the introduction within these spiritualistic circles of a person suffering from that rare ocular affection known as *nyctalopia* might have a tendency to break up such exhibitions; for patients thus affected see perfectly well in the darkness, and methinks most mediums would object to their presence, inasmuch as the conditions would not be favorable."

"No modern medium would knowingly submit to such a test," replied Athothis; "although I must admit that the idea is an admirable one, and the experiment well worth trying. However, you can have an immediate opportunity, as your spiritual vision will be far better in the dark *seance* we are about to enter than that of any sufferer from *nyctalopia*. But see! the blackness of night is rapidly increasing, and the spiritual apparitions are multiplying. Let us enter along with these ærial phantoms, these followers of Set. Doctor Diabolus is now communing, surrounded by a magical circle of misguided and terrified mortals. We shall be invisible to this arch necromancer, thanks to our stronger power, and likewise undisturbed by these pixies and goblins, whom I could banish by a mere motion of my sacred ank." So speaking, Athothis, followed by Paulus Androcydes, passed into the mansion.

Seated in a large and handsomely furnished parlor were twenty-eight mortals arranged in a circle, holding hands. In the center of this human ring were two figures—one a ghostly, shadowy form in white, the other a tall, cadaveric looking man, with high cheek-bones, narrow forehead, crooked nose, and a pair of green, feline-looking eyes, that ever and anon seemed to gleam with phosphorescence.

"Observe the varied expressions on the faces of these people," remarked Athothis. "Notice how their eyes are fastened on this white apparition, which is to them a messenger from the other world. Behold the rapturous smile on the face of the silver-haired old gentleman sitting at our left, who thinks he sees in this spirit a beloved daughter, lately deceased. He is a widower, and she was his only child. He is now waiting, hoping that the dear wife of his youth will also appear. Listen! the medium has ceased his miserable groaning, and is speaking."

"This spirit," declared the medium, "says that her name on earth was Emilie Bonneville, and that she passed away from this life five weeks since. She also states that the lady now materializing is her mother, who died when she was an infant. They desire to say that they are very, very happy, and are waiting to meet their father, who lingers on this side. Do any persons present recognize these spirits?"

"My wife! my daughter!" exclaimed the gray-haired gentleman, in tones of delight.

"The gentleman may shake hands with his family if

he desires," said Professor Diabolus, in an awe-inspiring voice ; " and I trust that there are no sceptics present to disturb this happy family reunion."

Profound silence fell over the room for a few seconds, then the two shadows disappeared.

" This is truly wonderful !" observed Paulus Andrceydes ; " and, strangest thing of all, I can read the thoughts of every person in this circle. For instance, that dark-eyed young man to the right is a journalist, who was inclined but a moment since to spring forward and seize the spirit."

" Such an attempt would have resulted in failure," replied Athothis ; " since the medium is also a mind reader. The apparitions you have just seen were so vaporous that a mere breath of air would have dissolved the aggregation of spiritual atoms. I am fully aware that most of these materialization performances are mere tricks in optical magic, carried on under cover of darkness by impostors, who often are so bungling as to be detected in fraud. Professor Diabolus, however, is an adept in this business, and has, no doubt, a diploma from the Druzes of Lebanon, who are the best modern practitioners of this art."

" Methinks this circle has more centers than allowed by Euclid, quoth Paulus Androcydes ; " for, besides the medium, I observe another form, and notice innumerable lights flitting around the apartment."

" Those are the gleaming eyes of demons, awaiting their turn to masquerade as the materialized forms of departed mortals," answered Athothis, smilingly.

" Musical instruments are suspended in the air without any respect for the law of gravitation ; bells are flying around and wildly ringing without the assistance of

human hands," murmured Paulus Androcydes, in spiritual amazement. " This is a marvelous performance, and
evidently Professor Diabolus is doing nothing except to
invoke these manifestations with heart-rending groans."

" He is a passive tool in the hands of Set," remarked
Athothis, in a tone of contempt. " He has bartered
away his chances for eternal life, and is used by these
demons in their wicked practices. His mind is already
affected, inasmuch as he deems himself a controller of
ghosts, when in fact he is a mere slavish subject of lost
angels. His shall be mental torment hereafter. For
know, mortal, that these false angels, personating the
good and true among the loved and departed, fill the
world with despair by giving bad advice, and are the
vilest of liars in the Court of the Prince of Darkness,
the cursed Set."

" Yet, these mortals are evidently pleased by the mes-
sages sent," said Paulus Androcydes ; " although, it is
true, the medium seems to be the mouthpiece through
which all communications are transmitted. But, see !
that beautiful girl in the circle is speaking to the shadow
standing by Professor Diabolus. Her mouth is wreathed
in smiles as she looks at the face of her dead mother
and whispers, ' My dear mamma ! you have made me so
happy by coming here again to-night ; and I no longer
doubt a future existence, and know that we shall meet
again. Oh ! mamma, have you nothing to say ?' "

" The spirit says her name in this life was Gertrude
Posey," groaned the medium, " and desires to advise her
daughter to avoid the person of whom she is thinking, if
she desires to be happy."

" Professor Diabolus is a villain !" cried Paulus Androcydes, indignantly. " This young lady was thinking

of a very clever clerk, a client of mine at times, who is a sober, honest, industrious man, and who would make her a good husband."

" Exactly !" remarked Athothis, with a grim smile. " Yet, the advice of the demon, now playing the *role* of affectionate mother, will be duly followed by this poor girl, who may marry some wretched scamp, and lead a horrible existence. But, see! another shadow has appeared, and is standing in front of your sceptical friend, the dark-eyed young journalist. He evidently believes now, as he is weeping."

" 'T is the living likeness of his mother !" exclaimed Paulus Androcydes. " She was my patient once, and died of chronic asthma. She was a gentle, kindly old lady, who read her Bible daily, but worshiped that boy. Listen to the words the wicked medium is putting in her mouth:

" Dear boy, your mother is ever near you. Keep on in your present path, and you will acquire fame and fortune. Ah! my child, things on this heavenly side of life are not what we were taught on earth. All here is beauty and divine love. I no longer am blinded by religious prejudices. Ah! my son, your mother was obliged to unlearn much that she was taught in the physical state. All now is light where formerly there was darkness. But I can say no more at present; I feel weak to-night." And with this the apparition disappeared.

" The base deceiver !" growled Paulus Androcydes, in a passion. " The demon who has assumed to represent this young man's mother, and thus mislead the youth, deserves severe punishment. I can now see the pernicious influences exerted by these destroyers of human happiness and reason; these crowders and pushers for insane asylums; these progenitors of future generations of demented ones. Yet, no wonder the young man was deceived, for the ghostly apparition just faded was the exact image of his deceased mother."

"Why say deceased, since the living can also be made to materialize and dematerialize?" said Athothis. "Do you desire to punish this medium and the next demon who enters?"

"Show me more of this magic," answered Paulus Androcydes, eagerly. "Let me be the agent for punishing these wicked beings."

"So be it," quoth Athothis. "For in order to convince you of my superior powers in magic, you shall pass through the body of this medium and demon, and, standing again at my side, see before you your own shadow. This is an experiment of ancient Egypt, but is best practiced in the full glare of the sun."

"Agreed!" exclaimed Paulus Androcydes, delighted to be made the subject of more experimentation. Yet, hardly had he uttered this word than, standing in the center of the circle, appeared his own form, moving about as in life. At the same instant the medium fell to the floor attacked with epilepsy. The circle broke up in confusion. The gas was turned on, and Medea, the wife of Professor Diabolus, knelt on the floor beside her now really suffering husband.

Athothis laughed at the dismay caused by this experiment, and quietly remarked: "Observe how the fallen angels have flown before my magic in terror. We are masters of the situation. But, see! your materialized shadow still moves about the apartment, and in order to punish the demon who is personating you, I must once more exert my power. *Hawthor, Mulika, Mah, Ra!*"

And as the Egyptian spoke these cabalistic words, the shadow of Paulus Androcydes disappeared, while a large brown bat flew wildly around the room in vain efforts to escape. "Now we can punish the demon with physical torture," continued Athothis. "Under the form of a bat he can be crushed, and never again will be capable of working mischief to mortals." And even as he made these remarks the terrified bat was crunched under the boot-heel of the gray-haired man. All was now confusion. The medium was carried to an adjoining chamber, and the mystified audience dispersed.

"I am strongly puzzled by these manifestations," said Paulus Androcydes.

"So others have been," responded Athothis.

"Yet, I have not yet learned how this magic is done," expostulated Paulus Androcydes. "I would fain witness more of these experimental tests. Explain this mystery, Oh! mighty Egyptian necromancer!"

"I will not," answered Athothis.

"You can not!" retorted Paulus Androcydes.

"He could, but he would not," replied Athothis, laughing merrily; "for, remember, with mediums, as with doctors, 'there are tricks in all trades but ours.'"

"Perhaps even you are a demon?" whispered Paulus Androcydes, musingly.

"Perhaps!" retorted Athothis, quietly. "Yet, if you desire to further investigate these phenomena, you can visit the *seances* of Professor Diabolus at some future time."

"I believe you are the devil!" cried Paulus Androcydes, angrily.

"The world is full of them," answered the Egyptian, sneeringly. "Yet, consider me a spirit of the first dynasty, and not a petty magician, like this modern medium. Come ! my mortal friend ! Time is too valuable to waste here. Come !" And once more Athothis and Paulus Androcydes drifted into the open air, leaving the mansion of Professor Diabolus far behind.

CHAPTER XVII.

IN WHICH ATHOTHIS AND PAULUS ANDROCYDES VISIT A
HANGING GARDEN IN UTOPIA, AND THE EGYPTIAN
BOLDLY CLAIMS THAT ALCOHOL IS THE INVENTION OF
SET.

THE moon was climbing the eastern horizon, and the night clear and star decked. The warm, balmy breath of spring kissed the perfumed lips of the modest violets, that played hide and seek under the mosses of the park.

"What a charming evening!" cried Paulus Androcydes, in tones of sincere delight. "Few cities in the world have as beautiful surroundings as Utopia. Look at the hill-tops, adorned with illuminated towers and palaces of pleasure, outlined against the azure sky like castles in tales of enchantment. See the town below, with its myriads of twinkling lights. Note the silver-frosted river, spanned by gracefully arched bridges, that cast on the bosom of the gently flowing waters the reflection of many green, red, and orange-colored lanterns, that sparkle like precious gems. Ah! this view is superb. Behold! the temples dedicated to music and art, and the—"

"Enough!" exclaimed Athothis, impatiently. "Utopia needs not your eulogy. But, I see a modern hanging garden, fashioned as those of ancient Babylon. Let us rest on this pinnacle for a few moments, and look down

14

on the throng of merry revelers, who, seated at long
tables, with clinking glasses of foaming nectar, keep
time to the sweet strains of harmony, borne to us on the
beer-haunted zephyrs."

"Why allude to beer and music in the same breath?"
asked Paulus Androcydes, with evident signs of spiritual
irritation.

"Because in Utopia the two seem inseparable," answered Athothis, smilingly.

" I suppose you will claim that the ancient Egyptians
had better beer than these moderns," quoth Paulus Androcydes, tauntingly. " Hast tasted the amber foam,
distilled here ?"

" No !" replied Athothis, firmly ; " nor do I care to touch
this delightful compound of spoiled rice, old corn, glucose,
and cocculus indicus, or perhaps stramonium and strychnia.   My spiritual palate rejects the potions of the age
with disgust.   Isis, who invented the process of extract-
ing pure grape juice—the real unfermented wine—would
never have handed a mug of your modern drink to her
beloved Osiris."

" You had no wine in Egypt of old," remarked Paulus
Androcydes ; " for Herodotus claims that no grapes were
grown in the Nile country, and that your liquors were
made from barley."

" I deny this statement !" said Athothis, indignantly.
" Herodotus was mistaken ; for, gaze at our most ancient
monuments and hieroglyphics at Memphis and Thebes,
that present representations of the preparation of wine
juice. The first fermented juice was invented long before
my day and generation, by that evil spirit, Set, who,
desiring to make whole races of people his slavish subjects, gave alcohol to the world, in order to create mad-

ness in the human brain, thus destroying reason and propagating crime."

"Pliny admits that the liquor of ancient Egypt was bad," observed Paulus Androcydes, in a tone of gentle sarcasm; "that it was made from corn-juice fermented in water, which leads the learned author to say that the Nile dwellers got drunk on corn-water."

"There are modern peoples who indulge in the same practice," responded Athothis, dryly; "but I boldly assert that for several centuries after my time the Egyptians did not drug their potions with additional poison to those already contained in fermented juices. They cared not to increase the toxic action of a known dangerous agent for the mere purpose of cheapening the cost of the product, in order to extend its use among the poor working classes. I must insist that in my time wines were unfermented and only used on the occasion of religious festivals."

"Unfermented wine is very disagreeable," remarked Paulus Androcydes, sneeringly; "and some time after your first transmigration Egyptian tastes changed, for Mareotic and Antyllian wines of later dynasties were highly extolled by epicures of the Nile country. You are, no doubt, aware that such a *bon vivant* as Athenæus has asserted that the ancient Egyptians were sadly given to drink, and only avoided the evil effects of liquors by eating cabbage as an antidote—a custom followed by some modern races to the present day. Do you know that cabbage seed used in wine or beer will prevent intoxication?"

"I never tried self-experimentation," answered Athothis, quietly, "and never cared for headaches. Perhaps you speak from experience?"

"I do, indeed," responded Paulus Androcydes, laughingly, "and confess to a decided liking for the good things of modern life, including wine and beer, and can assure you that nothing is better for *post-prandial* neuralgia than an infusion of cabbage seed, drunk like tea, while piping hot."

"Alas! poor stomach!" cried Athothis, pityingly. "Yet this is a simpler remedy than the morphine and chloral with which modern doctors antidote alcohol—agents which in themselves only tend to congest an already poisoned brain.

"I notice many Hebrews in the gathering below; and, strange spectacle, they are eating salt with butter and *wienerwurst*. Shades of Moses, behold! In place of the *tarosh* or unfermented wine these children of Israel are drinking *ya-yin*, and still more uncleanly beer."

"The liberal spirit of the age is breaking down the barriers of ancient superstition," said Paulus Androcydes, triumphantly. "This is a century of religious progress, and these Jews care not to be longer bound down by ignorant customs. The word *kosher* is now obsolete; for, lo! my Semitic friends swallow cove oysters with the same relish as they do hog sausage."

"This liberal spirit of the age seems to be, as in olden times, only the spirit of Set," retorted Athothis. "The voice of the prophet is no longer respected. The invocation of Micah, 'Thou shalt not drink wine,' is forgotten, and Isaiah's warning, 'Strong drink shall be bitter for them that use it,' goes unheeded; and yet they say within themselves, We had Abraham for a father."

"*Shalom Alechem!*" remarked Paulus Androcydes, chidingly.

"Shalom!" replied Athothis, bowing his head to the Orient.

"The modern Jew, like the modern Christian, laughs at his ancestors," continued Paulus Androcydes, "and to my mind both are better than the old bigoted stock."

"New wine in old bottles?" murmured Athothis.

"Precisely," answered Paulus Androcydes. "Let the Jews drink their wine and beer in peace, for they are to be congratulated on overcoming Egyptian prejudices; for you must admit that from times of greatest antiquity these Hebrews used wine on their altars; and, according to the Talmud, all songs of praise in the temple were sung with wine, and not the unfermented article either, for the Mishna states that it must be mixed with three parts of water in order to render the liquor less strong. Your modern Jew is not a Nazarite, and has forgotten the name of Rechabite."

"And likewise forgotten the wisdom of Solomon," replied Athothis; "that learned one who wrote: 'Who hath woes? Who hath sorrow? Who hath babbling? Who hath wounds? Who hath redness of the eyes? They that tarry long at the wine.' And adds: 'At last it biteth like a serpent and stingeth like an adder.' Another wise old Jew hath said: 'Woe unto them that rise up early in the morning that they may follow strong drink, that continue until night until wine inflame them.' The evils of alcohol were known and described as faithfully by these Jewish seers as by the Egyptians; for, remember, that intemperance antedates Christianity."

"I am a Christian by birth," exclaimed Paulus Androcedes, proudly, "and the founder of our belief had no silly prejudices. He not only drank wine himself, but likewise gave it to others to drink. His first miracle was

to convert water into wine ; his last advice to his disciples to drink to his memory.   As for St. Paul, he advised
Timothy, ' Drink no longer water, but a little wine for
the stomach's sake.'   Methinks I should have attended
this good saint's church were he preaching at the present
day."

"Such serious subjects do not admit of jocularity,"
remarked Athothis, reprovingly.   "Nevertheless, I am
forced to confess that the habit of drink is increased or
diminished by the religious beliefs of mortals.   Thus
Christian nations, following the teachings of their leaders,
seem the most addicted to intemperance."

"Cynicism is unbecoming an immortal of the first
dynasty!" answered Paulus Androcydes, scornfully.
"This appetite for drink is, according to my notion, a
natural instinct, inherited by many kinds of animals,
birds, and insects, as well as mankind.   I have seen flies
intoxicated on the sugar in whisky toddy, and pigs
drunk from cherries steeped in liquor.   I have known
monkeys, goats, and parrots to be exceedingly fond of
wine ; horses that could drink gallons of beer, and cows
that doted on the swill from alcohol distilleries."

"And the milk of such cows will poison children who
drink it," retorted Athothis.   "And allow me to assure
you that the babes of the first dynasty did not die from
the poisoned lacteal secretions of swill-fed cattle."

"It has been claimed," continued Paulus Androcydes,
" that races of savages have been decimated by drunkenness when forced in contact with Christian peoples.   I
make this remark, lest you insist that mere instinct is
not akin to human reason.   But these wild tribes of men
in Africa, Asia, and America had their intoxicating
drinks long before they ever heard of Christianity.   That

civilization begets intemperance is a popular fallacy, un-
supported by any reasonable proof. The Africans drank
palm wines and fermented fruit juices, and the American
Indians fermented maple and sugar-cane years before
seeing the noble Caucasian. Semi-civilized people, like
the Chinese, were once given to intemperance, if we are to
believe Confucius, who has written, 'Be not given to excess in the use of wine;' while his well beloved disciple,
Mencius, deplores the vice of drunkenness, classing it
among the five defects of filial piety. In those days
raki, made from red and white rice, previously fermented,
was the favorite tipple, though the Chinese likewise used
beans, sugar, and potatoes in making alcoholic liquors."

" The Chinese are really a temperate race," observed
Athothis, admiringly; " for that great reformer, Buddha,
whose doctrines spread far and wide through the Celestial
Empire, was a thorn in the side of Set, inasmuch as he
prescribed total abstinence ; and modern China feels to-
day the full benefits of this learned philosopher's teachings."

" Bah !" cried Paulus Androcydes, in a voice of commingled contempt and pity. " China is a barbarous
country, filled up with a cat-rat-opium-eating population ;
and surely you must agree with me that poppy juice is
more dangerous than grape juice. And speaking of
ancient tipplers reminds me that the Brahmans and other
religious East Indian sects fed their very deities on
strong drink—that sacred *soma*, composed of ferns, fermented with malt and milk. Then, later they possessed
another intoxicant—*sura*. The former was supposed to
contain the divine essence of Indra, to whom these pa-
gans sang their Vedic hymns, such as ' Come hither, O !
Indra, to our sacrifice ! Drink of the soma, O ! soma

drinker! Come hither, O! Indra, and intoxicate. thyself.'"

"But this evil was reformed by the later Code of Menu," said Athothis; "and these wise laws commanded temperance, and prescribed severe penalties for drunkenness, as, for instance, it states, 'Any twice born man, who has intentionally drunk spirits, through perverse delusions of mind, must drink spirits aflame, and atone for his offense by thus burning his body.' Liquors made from rice, sugar, or plants are strictly prohibited by this same code, and the people of India, like those of China, would be total abstinence races, were it not for the unholy spirit of Set, who, guiding the evil spirit of Great Britain, forces its alcohol and opium down the throats of what you are pleased to term semi-civilized peoples. If the sword of Mahomet carried temperance before the crescent, so the cannon of England carries intemperance before the cross."

"This is rank profanity!" exclaimed Paulus Androcydes, angrily. "Methinks you attempt to make a point at the expense of my religion."

"'Tis the fault of his followers," said Athothis, calmly; "for the doctrines he taught were sublime—the equality of souls before Patah. Yet, in modern times, woman is not considered the equal of man, although first at his birth and last at his sepulcher. Give the mothers, sisters, daughters, and wives a voice in the Government. Then will the spirit of Set be vanquished; then will the prophecy be fulfilled; for it is written, 'The heel of the woman shall crush the serpent's head.' This voice has echoed down the ages. The earnest midnight vigil—woman's prayers and woman's tears—shall triumph. Always the stronger, and never the weaker spiritual sex.

Man is but her offspring, and, though gray-haired, a baby at the breast. Like the faithful Isis she wanders in search of Osiris, and the birth of Horus, the new light, will follow."

"Still dealing in imagery?" queried Paulus Androcydes, mockingly. "I fear you are a woman-rights man, in the disguise of the first dynasty. But permit me to say that I fully agree with that talented author who contended that 'man is the whole world, and the breath of God; woman but the rib and crooked piece of man.' You remember the witty Voltaire, who insisted that ideas were like moustaches—men had them, women never. I trust to have entered my first real transmigration ere women are permitted to make laws for my Government. I am a firm advocate of the superior rights and privileges of men and shall continue to enjoy my mortal as much as I hope to enjoy my immortal life. Because my neighbor can not drink liquor without making a beast of himself, is that a valid reason for my abstaining?"

"You could set a good example," answered Athothis, gently. "You could thus encourage those who are weak-headed and faint-hearted."

"On the same principle that my neighbor cannot eat green apples without colic, whereas I suffer no inconvenience from the delicious fruit," quoth Paulus Androcydes.

"The comparison is unfair to your own stomach," retorted Athothis. "Like all your sex, you are utterly selfish. Every man, according to your idea, must work out his own salvation; permit the sale of alcohol and opium to go on unchecked, regardless of the wishes of

15

womankind; let the victims of these poisons go headlong to destruction, on account of your miserable commercial spirit. Yet, if a man jumps into water, you stretch forth your hand and strive to save him."

"I do not fancy your manner of argument," rejoined Paulus Androcydes. "If one were to follow your idea, there would be no pleasure in life. See the merry throng of happy people sitting around the tables, chatting and drinking. I care not to rob humanity of its joys; for, heaven knows, it hath many labors and sorrows. Greece and Rome are my ideal patterns, if you desire me to extol ancient manners and customs. I admire Bacchus! Give me that paradise of Ulysses, amid isles of eternal summer, 'where the vines bear wines from large clusters, and the showers of Jove nourish them.' Would I were imperial Cæsar, sipping Chian, Falernian, and Lesbian liquors. Youth, song, and wine are all that make this life bright. Let the world eat drink, and be merry, for to-morrow we die. But

> "'Who dreads to the dust returning?
>   Who shrinks from the sable shore,
> Where the high and haughty yearning
>   Of the soul, can sting no more?
> No! stand to your glasses steady;
>   This world is a world of lies;
> One cup to the dead already;
>   Hurrah! for the next that dies.'"

"You can not be in earnest?" expostulated Athothis. "Yet, such wild sentiments, even when not seriously expressed, make me sad. None know the evil effects of alcohol better than members of your profession, and those early authorities, whom you seem so fond of quoting, were fully acquainted with its poisonous effects.

Pliny, for instance, says : 'It reveals the secrets of the mind—one man is heard to disclose the contents of his will, another lets fall an expression of fatal import, and so fails to keep to himself words which will be sure to come home to him with a cut throat.' How many a man has met death in this fashion ?"

"Simeon Seth states that ' the immoderate use of wine dissolves the vital tone, depresses natural heat, and occasions apoplexy, epilepsy, and tumors of the body.'

"Avicenna insists that the free use of wine ' induces diseases of the liver and brain, and debilitates the nerves ; that—' "

"Stop !" cried Paulus Androcydes. "These writers speak of persons who use such divine liquors in excess. Hippocrates was a lover of good liquors. Celsus calls them the good juices. Paulus Ægineta asserts that they give gladness and pleasure to the soul. Rhazes proclaims that wine warms the stomach and liver, and thus brightens the mind."

"But no man drinks wine in moderation," interrupted Athothis. "If he drink it at all, he doth it in such a manner as to experience the toxic effects. It is the gradual and increasing love for liquor that can not be conquered by the victim of Set. Philosophers may discourse learnedly of moderation, yet poets will sing the praises of the garlanded cup. Divines will preach a temperance they do not practice, while doctors will continue to prescribe alcohol along with the rest of poisons. The evils wrought by alcohol can never be estimated save by its real inventor, Set. Blighted hopes, woman's tears, broken hearts, cruel fears ; man's despair, mother's moans, poverty, and children's groans."

"Enough of this twaddle !" exclaimed Paulus Andro-

cydes, scornfully. "Gaze at the happy crowd below,
which, as time flies, becomes gayer and more reckless.
Ah! my Egyptian friend,

> "'Good wines the gift that God hath given,
>   To man alone beneath the heaven,
>   Of dance and song the genial sire,
>   Of friendship gay and soft desire.'

"Remember the advice of that giddy-headed Athenian
physician, Mnesitheus, who recommends occasional hard
drinking, as it produces purging and a certain relaxation.
You quoted Rabelais this morning, who contended that
drunkenness was better than physic, inasmuch as there
were more old drunkards than old physicians. Come!
let us inhale more of the delicious aroma arising from this
commingling perfume of whisky, wine, and beer."

"The vapory fumes of the liquor have already affected
your silly spiritual head,'' answered Athothis. "Jest no
more! for I see that the modern doctor knows the advantages of alcohol to his own business. Let the wholesale
poisoning of mankind proceed. Below, in the city, I
perceive the many colored lights of a modern pharmacy.
There we can investigate undisguised poisons." So saying, the spirits circled down from the lofty tower and
alighted on a public street.

CHAPTER XVIII.

IN WHICH THE SPIRITS VISIT A MODERN PHARMACY, AND
PAULUS ANDROCYDES DISCOVERS THAT THE LABEL ON
A BOTTLE IS NO SURE INDICATION OF THE CONTENTS.

THE brilliantly lighted shop, in front of which the
spirits paused, stood on a prominent street
corner, and was half surrounded by immense
plate-glass windows, adorned with curious
shaped flagons containing green, yellow, purple, and red
fluids of mysterious composition. In these windows were
also show-cases filled with perfumery, toilet powder, hair
brushes, combs, soap, tobacco, and cigars; while hung
around, for additional decorative purposes, were many
cheap colored, flashy advertisements, conceived in the
style of the modern French classical school, that served
to attract the attention of the honest citizen. One of
these pictures represented Venus before a modern dressing bureau, combing her long, wavy tresses, on which
was printed "Use Madame Tonsorial's Hair Restorer."
Another chromo exhibited a portrait of Ajax defying the
bilious lightning by covering his liver with a non-con-
ducting magnetic pad. There were other similar signs
too numerous to mention.

"This is our modern drug-store," said Paulus Androcydes, proudly. "Methinks you had nothing like it in
ancient Egypt."

"You are right," answered Athothis, with a humorous
twinkle in his spiritual orbs. "Our physicians com-

pounded their own medicines, and therefore knew precisely what was given the sick. But let us enter!" As these words were uttered the spirits passed into the store through a speaking trumpet, inscribed "For night calls."

"What a wonderful crystal palace is this!" exclaimed the Egyptian, in tones of feigned delight, as he gazed about in mock admiration at the immense array of glass bottles and china jars, adorned with cabalistic inscriptions. "This is the charmed laboratory of some skillful chemist and dealer in rare remedies, since the shelves fairly groan under the weight of an infinite variety of drugs and chemicals. Look at the honesty of the proprietor, too, for back of his dispensing case I observe the ominous sign, 'Beware of Poisons.'"

"Yes," answered Paulus Androcydes, laughingly; "I notice the druggist, Professor Prescriber, is now showing two of his friends the subtile qualities contained in a cut-glass bottle, labeled 'Pure French Brandy.' They are clinking glasses in order to ascertain whether the fluid is soluble in water. Heavens! Professor Prescriber is evidently intoxicated, as he is making a mistake in the prescription before him; and, in place of putting ten grains of sulphate of quinine in a powder, has substituted, through drunken carelessness, the same amount of morphine. That sickly-looking woman in front of the counter is waiting for the medicine. She is suffering from malaria, and the error in compounding will cost her her life. I must and will save her!"

"Nonsense!" remarked Athothis, laughing at the futile spiritual attempt of his comrade to grasp the powder. "Let the poison do its painless work! She is only a shop-girl, and is slowly being killed by her employer, who obliges his female clerks to stand on their feet twelve hours a day, waiting on the more fortunate sister-hood, who ride in luxurious carriages—those fashionable butterflies who patronize the murderers of their own sex."

"This is horrible!" exclaimed Paulus Androcydes, in agitation. "Yet, I have every reason to believe that such accidents are common in drug-stores, and that many of our patients die from the remedy instead of the disease. One of those gentlemen just drinking with the pharmacist is Doctor Enticer, who boasts he never took a glass of liquor in a bar-room; the other tippler is a president of a large bank. Prescriber is a cunning man, and, it is said, makes more money out of poor whisky than any person in Utopia."

"Do modern people trust druggists who run bar-room pharmacies?" asked Athothis, grimly.

"They do," responded Paulus Androcydes. "For Prescriber is a fat, jolly, whole-souled fellow, who is willing to prescribe for every person."

"What!" exclaimed Athothis. "Does the modern apothecary play the part of doctor?"

"He does!" answered Paulus Androcydes, "and is willing to give a remedy for every known ailment on demand. Indeed, many citizens think he possesses more real knowledge than a doctor, and trust implicitly in his advice."

"Strange!" murmured Athothis. "Yet, his shop is neat, clean, and attractive—things sadly lacking in most physician's offices. But speaking of drugs reminds me that much deceit and fraud is being practiced here; for, on investigating these numerous jars and vials, I find that their contents do not correspond with the labels. Thus this jar, marked 'Gum Acacia,' contains only gum feronia, admixed with dextrine. This drug was never derived from the plant that Strabo mentions as forming a hedge around the Temple of Osiris at Acanthus; and Theophrastus would never identify this article as his favorite gum arabic. Observe the jar marked ' Myrrh;' this is not the fine drug known by the Egyptians and Jews, and mentioned in the Old Testament. The ancient variety was an emblem of purity; this medicine is now unrefined and adulterated with bedellium and cherry gum. Look at this pot of opium! It is totally unlike our ancient Egyptian extract, which was not mixed with resin, sugar, and starch. Avicenna and Rhazes would never have advocated the use of this variety. Behold! this Salep, which is formed of colchicum tubers and corn starch. This sample would not have a different effect on man than on woman, like the article prescribed by Dioscorides. This vial, labeled ' Bitter Almonds,' contains only peach kernels, while the bottle of ' Oil of Bitter Almonds ' is merely lard oil and mirbane. Such almonds were not the kind sent to Egypt by Jacob, in order to ransom his son. Notice the aniseed. that once famous diuretic, now constituted of conium maculatum and sand. This modern asafetida is one half resin; this colocynth the fruit of a different curcurbitallous plant; these squills are not the sort described by Pythagoris in a special monograph; these aloes are not the Red Sea kind, known by Galen. Haly Abbas would have scorned such specimens of senna leaves, and would have called them *cassia brevipes*. This pomegranate rind would never have suited Rhazes for an anthelmintic. Here is ginger, such as Ægineta never described. What would Celsus have said to this scammony, if he desired to destroy a tape-worm? scammony made of tragacanth, yolk of eggs, and old resin! Herodotus would have laughed this cinnamon to scorn. This honey is not from Mount Hymettus, but from glucose. Ah! here is a small boy leaning over the counter, and asking for a few pennies' worth of castor oil. Strange that children have used castor oil since the first dynasty. Surely, such a cheap drug must be pure. What! can it be possible that the modern variety is lard, with a little croton oil? The small boy is now asking for a marsh-mallow drop as a premium for his patronage. However, this contains no althæa, which is fortunate, considering the action ascribed by Xenocrates to that drug. Shades of ye ancient physicians of Egypt, Greece, Rome, and Arabia! No wonder that the modern doctor fails to obtain the same remedial results from drugs as his medical ancestors; for the medicine of to-day differs widely from that of the honest olden times. Methinks that the chemist makes his own physic, and no longer depends on nature's laboratory."

"You slander the noble profession, of which Prescriber is an honest member," said Paulus Androcydes, in a tone of vexation. "I am willing to admit, however, that the drugs of ancient times are gradually disappearing before our chemical establishments, which find handsomer profits in manufacturing than in importing pure medicines. The modern chemist now supplies the market with refined agents, in place of the crude remedies of former ages."

"True!" responded Athothis. "Chemistry is now the principal aid to the physician. Art has supplanted Nature in supplying medicine for mankind; the bountiful gifts offered by Patah are rejected for those presented by mortals. But, since you believe in the unadulterated purity of chemically prepared agents, cast your spiritual glance over these numerous modern prepared medicines, and make a rapid mental analysis."

"Then," answered Paulus Androcydes, in the manner of the ordinary trance medium: "I see before me—

> "Acetic acid, containing sulphuric and hydrochloric acid;
> Calomel, in which there is corrosive sublimate;
> Bitartrate of potash, mixed with calcium tartrate;
> Benzoic acid, of cinnamic acid and vinegar;
> Citric acid, adulterated with oxalic acid and iodium;
> Iodide of potassium, one-half bromide of potassium;
> Morphine, one-third quinine;
> Quinine, three-fourths cinchonidia;
> Santonin, two-thirds boracic acid;
> Tartrate of iron, of calcium, dextrine, and milk sugar;
> Chloral, of chloral alcoholates;
> Glycerine, mixed with glucose and mucilage;
> Copaiba, of turpentine, resin, and gurjun balsam."

"Are you satisfied?" demanded Athothis.

"I am simply amazed," answered Paulus Androcydes. "But let me investigate these powders, as drugs in this form are most easily adulterated, and the impurity more liable to escape detection. Great heavens! I see before me—

> "Powdered rhubarb, one-half sea biscuit and curcuma;
> Mustard, made of starch, red pepper, and tumeric;
> Gamboge, colored tartrate of lime;
> Linseed, of cake meal;
> Cubebs, of black pepper and chaff;
> Lycopodium, from pine pollen and dextrine;
> Manna, of glucose and flour;
> Cinchona, of red bark;
> Musk, three-fourths sea biscuit;
> Arrow root, nothing but Tacca starch;
> Tapioca, made of clear potato starch.

"And the essential oils—'Angels and ministers of grace defend us!'

> Oil of anise, mixed with turpentine;
> Oil of cade, common tar and juniper;
> Oil of lemon, one-half turpentine;
> Oil of sandal, one-half castor oil;
> Olive oil, nothing but cotton-seed oil.

"Can it be possible that Professor Prescriber deals in such vile compounds? But, look! here is

> 'Sulphur, one-half gypsum;
> Saffron, calendula flowers, dyed with Campeachy wood;
> Dandelion, two-thirds chicory;
> Hydrastin, of beet root, serpentaria, and meal;
> Capsicum, Venetian red and brick dust admixed;
> Cardamom, adulterated with orange seed."

"Hold!" cried Athothis. "Do not exhaust the whole pharmacopœia."

"Can it be that any of my patients have taken such remedial agents?" asked Paulus Androcydes, anxiously.

"Not only possible, but more than probable," answered Athothis; "for, following the commercial spirit of the age, such substitution is common. Nor would the druggist who sells patent medicine hesitate at such trifles as adulterations. Besides, your people are to blame, as they patronize the apothecary who sells cheapest. I am willing to admit that a few honest, capable druggists still live, but the mass are like our friend Professor Prescriber, and buy goods from unscrupulous dealers, who employ skillful compounders. Another thing I wish to observe is, that your modern doctor is at fault for this sad state of affairs; for, believe me, not one physician in a hundred knows any thing of botany or pharmacy. The vast mass of practitioners would be totally unable to recognize even a few of the drugs they daily prescribe."

"Are all the medicines in this store impure?" demanded Paulus Androcydes.

"They are about as free from adulterations as those we have already noticed," responded Athothis.

At this moment two small children—one a boy, the other a girl—entered the store, and walked up to a counter, ornamented with a marble fountain, marked "Pure Soda and Genuine Fruit Syrups."

"Poor babies!" said Paulus Androcydes, pityingly. "I have seen the evil effects of these vile manufactured mineral waters and syrups on the infantile digestive apparatus.

"How the fluid sparkles and foams!" remarked Athothis. "Children under the first dynasty indulged in no beverages, save milk and water. They call this liquid soda; yet it contains no soda, and is only distilled water, surcharged with gas, created from sulphuric acid and marble dust, while the pure fruit syrup, supplied to these children of the people, is nothing but chalk and glucose, flavored with tonka bean, and colored with red analine. It is poison!"

"The little ones have been to the corner grocery," said Paulus Androcydes; "for they have a market basket and a tin can for milk. See the character of food furnished moderns. These children have bought

"One pound of coffee—half roasted beans and chicory;
One pint of milk—half hydrant water;
Two pounds of sugar—one half glucose;
One paper of pepper—two thirds gypsum and starch;
One pound of lard—containing tallow;
One pound of butter—pure oleomargarine;
Two loaves of bread—really! pure.

" These children belong to some laborer. Their father is probably a poor devil, who works twelve hours a day, and is so ignorant as not to know that half of what he buys is fraudulent."

" Yes," retorted Athothis; " their parents wonder why the children do not grow fat and healthy with such an abundance of food."

" Who can reform this terrible state of affairs?" cried Paulus Androcydes, despairingly.

" When the moral sense is cultivated as much as the modern commercial instinct, these matters will be reformed," replied Athothis.

" Let us leave this place," murmured Paulus Androcydes. " My spiritual heart is heavy."

" Ha! ha! ha!" laughed Athothis, as they fairly spun through the air. " I would teach you much, could I but tarry with you a few hours longer, but my time is almost up."

CHAPTER XIX.

THE SPIRITS ATTEND THE OPERA OF AIDA, AND ATHO-
THIS, AFTER INVEIGHING AGAINST THE COSTUMES OF
THE PERIOD, FALLS IN LOVE WITH A MODERN SINGER,
AND DISAPPEARS FOREVER WITH AMNERIS.

HE full, silvery rays of moonlight fell softly
over the city as the spirits once more rested in
the upper ether.

"Bright orb of night! thou seemest to smile
on earth, as if in token of a benediction," said Athothis, reverently glancing upward.

"You are growing sentimental," whispered Paulus
Androcydes, smilingly. "'T is a glorious evening, however, and I wonder not at your enthusiasm. Behold!
the glittering diamonds on the bosom of heaven. It
must have been on such a night that the young stars
sang together the music of the spheres; and, speaking
of harmony, reminds me that a fine opera company will
presently commence the performance of Aida, in the
magnificent building below. Would you like to witness
an Egyptian play, performed by moderns?"

"Nothing would be more pleasing!" responded Athothis, eagerly. "Nothing is more charming to a spirit
than music, and I fain would listen to entrancing melody,
providing I am not obliged to be one of the performers."

"Are you a musician?" asked Paulus Androcydes, in

evident curiosity. "Methought music was but little understood in the first years of the world."

"Mothers sang lullabies to the first babes of humanity," answered Athothis. "The origin of melody dates back to the very dawn of creation, and all nature then as now was filled with delicious sounds. As regards my ability in the performing line, know, mortal, that I have sung as a nightingale in Persia, as a canary in Germany, as a mocking-bird in America."

"I suppose you have met some of the earlier poets and singers during your many transmigrations!" quoth Paulus Androcydes, indulging in a vein of spiritual sarcasm.

"Yes," replied Athothis, seriously. "I met Solomon about five centuries since; he was croaking in a frog concert given for the Benefit of the Queen of Sheba, in a lotus pond near the great pyramid. As for King David, I saw him about twenty years ago in the Zoological Garden at Hamburg. He was a captive parrot, serenading Uriah's wife, who was a brown Brazilian monkey, confined in an adjoining cage."

"Can it be possible that Solomon and David are still transmigrating?" queried Paulus Androcydes.

"Even so," responded Athothis. "They are still living and striving to master the music of the future."

"Yours is a strange doctrine," said Paulus Androcydes, laughingly. "Perhaps Shakespeare was a believer, since he wrote—

> "'All the world's a stage,
> And all the men and women merely players.
> They have their exits and their entrances,
> And one man in his time plays many parts.' "

"His was a master mind!" exclaimed Athothis, in

tones of sincere admiration. "I encountered him ten years since in Denmark, where, on the moss-covered battlements of an ancient castle, he was rehearsing Hamlet in company with a strolling party of chirping black crickets. 'T was on such a night as this, and I played the Ghost to his melancholy Prince."

"Perhaps you have met Ananias and Sapphira during some of your innumerable change artist performances?" remarked Paulus Androcydes, in concealed spiritualistic merriment.

"I have, indeed," murmured Athothis, softly; "they are ubiquitous in the present age. But to change the subject, seeing that you doubt the veracity of many of my statements, suppose we enter this chaste temple dedicated to music. I observe that the 'free list is suspended,' but that's one of our advantages in the spiritual state; having no money, being real dead heads. Come in!" And a second later they occupied the best private box, overlooking the orchestra and stage.

"This is a grand audience," whispered Paulus Androcydes, as he gazed at the sea of upturned faces, and listened to the flutter of thousands of perfumed and undulating fans, whose fascinating movement caused artificial currents of fragrance in the upper hall. "Look at this gorgeous dressing, my Egyptian friend! You must admit that the costumes of the present day are much more becoming and stylish than those of the first dynasty?"

"I regret to differ with you again," answered Athothis. "Although willing to acknowledge that differences in temperature govern what you term style, Egypt was and still is a tropical country, and many of my people were contented with the fashionable garment of that age.

The primitive dress was a leaf, and to-day most fashionable dresses are fabricated from a material derived from a worm that feeds on leaves; so feminine costume is yet indirectly Eve-like. Yes, all these handsome silks are the result of a transmigration; a worm feeds on leaves, weaves its cocoon, becomes a chrysalis, changes to a butterfly, and flits about in royal attire, to the delight of the children of mankind."

"I know full well that silk is the result of a metamorphosis," answered Paulus Androcydes, petulantly. "Ah! my Egyptian friend, you carry your peculiar doctrine too far. Transmigration even in dress! What a wild absurdity!"

"But even this little example must prove the soundness of my views," retorted Athothis "for you must acknowledge that the larva, pupa, and moth, although widely different in form and manner of living, are nevertheless one and the same organism existing under varied conditions. I notice that moderns, like ancients, utilize all kinds of substances for self-adornment, and often clothe themselves in the former earthly skins of their ancestors. I see in this audience the fragmentary remains of insects, animals, birds, fishes, and plants, which, for the sake of quieting conscience, are called silk, bone, fur, leather, feathers, pearls, linen, muslin, and cotton—a formula the ingredients of which, when properly compounded and added to woman, make a dame of fashion."

"You are not only unreasonable, but ungallant," observed Paulus Androcydes, in a tone of vexation. "All moderns have a highly cultivated sense of modesty, and our polite society would be sadly shocked at the primeval costume, except when noticed in pictures and statuary.

Besides, in this climate we would perish from cold, were it not for our artificial outer coverings, which, although made from various fabrics, are absolutely necessary to protect health. Even in a spiritual state clothing seems essential, since your own princely form is invested in the dematerialized drapery of the first dynasty."

"We arrayed ourselves in fine linen and other vegetable textures even in my time," replied Athothis. "Yet, men and women did not deform their bodies as now. Your proud and arrogant Caucasians laugh the Mongolians to scorn, because forsooth they make women's feet small by artificial methods; yet your people contract their brains with tight hats, and induce epilepsy and imbecility among your infants by contracted head coverings. Look at those gentlemen passing down the central aisle in search of seats, carrying their silken helmets in their hands. Methinks the classical Greek and Roman warriors would expire from laughter on seeing such card-board imitations of metallic crown protectors. Such articles of costume provoke baldness and neuralgia."

"You should read Foville," interrupted Paulus Androcydes, "and would, no doubt, agree with him as to the injurious effects of modern European head coverings. Notice how the close-fitting neckties and collars worn by these men and women interfere with the circulation of the blood between the head and heart, creating a venous stasis. Look at the prominent and projecting Caucasian eye. My people are subjects of apoplexy, vertigo, and nose-bleed; for the carotid arteries are constantly forcing blood in the cerebrum, and its prompt return to the lungs and heart is prevented by our close collars and cravats. Behold our modern tight-fitting

coats, vests, and dresses, which interfere with respiration, by contracting the expansion of the chest and abdomen. No wonder the wearers of such costumes pant
in distress for want of oxygen, and die of consumption
by the millions. The faces and hands of this audience
are tense and swollen, and we seek our relaxations to
pleasure in garments of fashion, that smother and dis-
comfort their wearer. Our men and women squeeze
their feet and hands in contracted and ill-fitting boots
and shoes, while our girls are pinched in steel corsets."

"Good!" cried Athothis, approvingly. "You will
presently agree with me that modern attire is gotten up
wholly in the interest of the medical profession. Your
doctors, in fact, are molding every thing to serve their
own ends. These ladies' corsets especially cause many
feminine complaints—cancers, tumors."

"Hush!" said Paulus Androcydes. "Do not speak so
loud, lest the lady in the box below may overhear even
the spiritual observation, and become uneasy. But these
corsets are a very old invention; for even Galen decried
the use of such instruments of torture. The modern dame
of fashion merely imitates her Greek cousin, who donned
the *sefosdone*, and her Roman cousin, who wore the *castula*.
All medical writers of antiquity inveigh against the com-
pression of woman's abdomen by *faciæ*; but the gentler
sex ever desired to make their hips appear broader.
But, blessed be the memory of Catherine de Medicis,
the true inventor of the modern appliance known as the
whalebone stay, and praised be Bouvier, the historian of
the corset; but cursed, thrice cursed be J. J. Rosseau,
that savage critic of feminine underwear. Yet, you
must remember that the vast majority of the maids and
matrons, comprising this audience, are idle creatures, of

sedentary habits, who exercise so seldom that their muscles are flabby and atrophied; elegant and refined beauties, who can not ride or walk without the artificial support of these steel and whalebone appliances."

"I notice," remarked Athothis, musingly, "that your modern feminine livers are indented, and stomachs and other more important viscera displaced, by this health-destroying contrivance."

"Hist!" exclaimed Paulus Androcydes. "As I observed before, our conversation may be overheard. Surely you would not wish to do away with our modern feminine backaches, headaches, vertigo, hysteria, dyspepsia, cancers, tumors, displacements, consumption, etc. Do you wish to destroy the business of our obstetricians and gynæcologists?"

"I see the point," answered Athothis, grimly. "Fashion has ever been one of the best patrons of physic."

"Observe the blushes on the cheeks of yonder girl," said Paulus Androcydes. "I sincerely trust that she has not listened."

"Her blushes are purchased by the box," replied Athothis, smilingly. "Her golden tresses were imported. Her luminous eyes are truly beautiful. An Italian might remark of her, *Bella-donna*. Her teeth were never cast in nature's mold. Her complexion is made of arsenic internally and bismuth violet powder on the epidermis. But, hark! the music has commenced; the curtain has risen. Can it be? Oh! glorious Egypt, my country! Dear land of my nativity! Is this a dream or is it reality?"

The Egyptian leaned forward, gazing in spiritual rapture on the opening scene in "Aida;" for there, before his delighted vision, was the grand hall in the Palace of

Memphis, with its broad colonnades on either hand adorned with statuary and flowers, while in the dim distance loomed the wondrous pyramids.

"At last you have discovered something modern that is pleasing!" murmured Paulus Androcydes, exultingly, as he observed the smile of pleasure on the Egyptian's face.

"I am very, very happy!" exclaimed Athothis. "I am overwhelmed with joy. Memphis was my home during many transmigrations, and this stage effect is so artistic and realistic that my spiritual imagination may easily deceive me. I shall give myself up to the full enjoyment of this operatic performance. Shades of Isis! Behold the lovely daughter of Egypt who is now singing! At last, after the lapse of ages, I have found my true affinity within the mortal frame of this actress."

"What!" said Paulus Androcydes, in a tone of disgust and astonishment; "a prince of the first dynasty in love with a modern singer? This woman is no Egyptian; she merely plays the part of Amneris. She is madly in love with Radmes, who will presently forsake her for Aida, a captive African slave."

"She is a king's daughter," replied Athothis, in a tremulous voice. "She loves him not! I read her mind clearly. She is dreaming as she sings of the glories of Egypt. Weary and heart-sick, tired out with endless toil before the footlights, she seeks rest in imagination, and her mind soars with her voice heavenward. She feels my unseen presence; and, listen! she is singing—

> "'Has not another vision,
>   One more sweet, more enchanting,
>   Found favor in your heart?'

"No, mortal! Radmes is not my rival; for presently

the spirit of Amneris shall leave her body, and hence-
forth dwell with me."

"Do you mean that she shall die on the stage in order
that her soul may meet your spirit?" demanded Paulus
Androcydes. "Yet, how can this be, since she must
submit to the same transmigration as other mortals?"

"She is mine forever," replied Athothis, joyously.
"Know, mortal, that I have godlike power, and Amneris, like many other women, shall be saved from painful
transmigration through her innate faith."

"Strange spirit!" gasped Paulus Androcydes. "Why
should an immortal fall in love at first sight?—that, too,
with a mere play actress and opera singer."

"Sneer not at the profession of my Amneris," responded Athothis. "She is merely playing the part
assigned to her in the order of nature. She is too beautiful to tarry longer on earth, and I shall bear her away
at the end of the last act. Amneris, my angel, I adore
thee!"

"I am bitterly disappointed in you, my Egyptian
friend," said Paulus Androcydes, mournfully. "Yet, on
consideration, it does not excite my wonder, since this
is the first time in six thousand years that you have had
a chance to fall in love with a woman. It is said that
Terra and Chaos were the parents of love—long before
even the gods were acquainted with that passion—and
there has been no accounting for tastes since Venus
wedded the ugly Vulcan. Perhaps you are Jupiter,
again seeking a sweetheart in the disguise of a satyr,
bull, swan; and I suppose you will presently disappear
in a golden shower, your outgoing being as mysterious as
your incoming. Yet, methinks your love for this singer
is as foolish as that of the moon for Endymion. Perhaps

you are one of those Telchines who figure so largely in the fables of the Platonists; or you may be one of those wicked spirits mentioned by Herodotus as haunting the sacred temple at Babylon, at the invitation of the Chaldean magi."

"Silence, mortal!" cried Athothis, haughtily. "Know that I am a prince of royal blood, and my love is pure and not of the modern kind."

"Yet, I can not understand how one in your highly organized spiritual state should be enamored with a mortal woman," replied Paulus Androcydes. "As for me, I might transmigrate from sphere to sphere for millions on billions of centuries, and never experience a real feeling of love for one of the opposite sex. So far, I have lived single and unmated; so let me remain a bachelor in other planets."

"She will come to you when least expected," whispered Athothis, gently. "She will enter your heart as Amneris has mine. So love shall lead you captive."

Thus they discoursed of the tender passion and of music, and the opera moved on; while at each moment Athothis felt the soul of Amneris filling him with divine joy. They listened entranced to the "*Gloria all Egitto!*" beholding the triumphal procession of gorgeously robed kings and princesses, priests, warriors, and slaves. They watched the airy movements of the graceful dancing girls, and Paulus Androcydes even sighed softly when one of the *ballet* seemed to be looking directly at him. Presently a hymn of praise burst forth. "'T is the voice of my people from far-off Egypt," muttered Athothis, reverently bowing his head; and even as he inclined to the Orient the chorus sang:

> " Hail, mighty Patah !
> Spirit of life !
> Lo ! we invoke thee,
> Oh ! mighty Patah !
> Of earth the creator !
> Lo ! we invoke thee."

And the Egyptian priests, the magi, clad in the splendid robes of the temple, chanted and chanted, with eyes looking heavenward.

> ' Hail, thou great maker
> Of earth and heaven !
> Lo ! we invoke thee !
> Life of the universe !
> Oh ! love eternal !
> Lo ! we invoke thee !"

" Farewell, forever !" cried Athothis to Paulus Androcydes. " Listen ! Radmes is singing—

> " ' Morir si pura bella,
> Morir per me d' amore,
> Degli anni tuoi nel fiore,
> Fugir la vita.'

" Let these words be mine to Amneris."

" Stay !" exclaimed Paulus Androcydes, alarmed at the strange emotion displayed by the Egyptian. " Stay, mighty necromancer, do not desert me ! Restore me to the habitation from which you seduced me by false promises. Give me back my body !"

" Coward !" retorted Athothis. " To desire mortality after what you have undergone ! Do not cling to me ! Unhand me, ungrateful man ! See ! Amneris is calling me. She has thrown herself on the stone of the sacred vault, and is singing—

> " ' Peace everlasting, immortal love,
> Isis relenting, smiles from above.'

"Amneris! Amneris! Mine eternally!"

At this instant Paulus Androcydes appeared to fairly fly through space, spinning in the atmosphere with such extreme velocity that sparks seemed to flash from his eyes. Up! up! up! up! up! Down! down! down! Over rivers, hills, valleys, plains; rushing through ethereal cloudlets like a meteor, until he was blind from vertigo and fright. Horrible pains twinged each spiritual nerve and muscle—grinding pains, tearing pains, crushing pains—until, with a wild scream of mortal agony and a terrible thump, *he awoke!*

17

CHAPTER XX.

WAS IT A DREAM OR WAS IT REALITY?

YES! Paulus Androcydes awoke. The white ashen embers were cold on the hearth. He looked upward, and saw that the light in the antique hanging lamp was extinguished; then, raising his aching body from the floor, noticed, through the open window, the first gray streaks of early dawn.

www.ingramcontent.com/pod-product-compliance
Lightning Source LLC
Chambersburg PA
CBHW031058280326
41928CB00049B/1042